Football Stories
From the Boardroom to the Bootroom

collected and edited by
FREDDIE LONGE

LYON BELL

I'm delighted to introduce this book of stories and anecdotes as told by some of the most distinguished people in football. Royalties will be donated to Meningitis Research Foundation, a charity that funds crucial projects towards the understanding, preventing and treating of meningitis and septicaemia.

My sincere thanks to all the eminent people who took the time and trouble to contribute to this fantastic project and worthy cause. Whilst their involvement is not an endorsement of the charity, it is a much-appreciated gesture of goodwill and they deserve as much credit for their charitable work as they do for their fine reputations in football.

Special thanks also to the efforts of Charlie Wade, Jamie Emsell, Sarah Campbell and Will Price, and James Barker at Sports Business International.

Freddie Longe

Copyright © Freddie Longe, 2005
Illustrations © Alex Hughes

First published in 2005 in
Great Britain by
Lyon Bell Books (Publishers) Ltd of
Units 11 and 12 Common Lane North, Beccles
Suffolk NR34 9BN

The moral right of the author has been asserted

A catalogue record of this book is available from the British Library

ISBN: 0-9548806-1-7 (HB)

Cover design and typesetting by Dual Creative

Printed and bound in England by William Clowes Ltd

Meningitis Research Foundation

Meningitis and septicaemia are devastating diseases which can kill in hours. Although anyone of any age can get the diseases, babies, children and young people are most at risk.

Meningitis Research Foundation's vision is a world free from meningitis and septicaemia.

The charity funds research to prevent meningitis and septicaemia, and to improve survival rates and outcomes. The Foundation promotes education and awareness to reduce death and disability, and give support to people, through the Freefone 24-hour helpline 080 8800 3344.

We are delighted to be benefiting from the sales of 'Football Stories: From the Boardroom to the Bootroom'. I would like to thank Freddie Longe for the hours of work he has spent in compiling the fascinating anecdotes and to everyone who buys a copy. Special thanks also to all those who kindly contributed with anecdotes and stories making it possible to raise vital funds. Without support like this, Meningitis Research Foundation would not be able to carry out its crucial funding of research, raising awareness of the symptoms of meningitis and septicaemia and supporting those who have been affected.

Denise Vaughan

Denise Vaughan
Chief Executive
Meningitis Research Foundation

In association with

The Daily Telegraph

The Daily Telegraph is very excited to be associated with this unique collection of football stories from some of the legends of the game over the last fifty years. We support Meningitis Research Foundation and hope that our involvement through our newspaper and website will increase book sales and royalties to what is a very worthwhile charity.

Foreword

My career was just taking off at Manchester United when I was suddenly hit with viral meningitis. I was a super-fit nineteen year old with a promising career in front of me and it came as a massive shock when I was suddenly diagnosed. I remember waking up one night with breathing difficulties and before I knew it I was in hospital. I had to have lumber punctures, a test that involves the removal of spinal fluid from the base of the spine. It was horrendous but I was very lucky to make a complete recovery. Charities like Meningitis Research Foundation fund projects to improve the detection and treatment of these diseases. It is through their hard work and dedication that many young people, including myself, have been restored to full health. It is their aim to rid the world of both meningitis and septicaemia and therefore it's an honour to provide an introduction to this book of football stories which is raising money to help fund their continued efforts. I wish it every success.

Lee Sharpe

Ex Manchester United and England

Contents

Behind the Scenes

John Madejski

John Madejski is a successful businessman who built and sold the Auto Trader publishing empire. Worth a reputed £270m, he has learnt first hand what an expensive hobby football can be.

I decided to save Reading Football Club in 1990, when the liquidators were knocking on the door. I thought it would be nice to put something back into the area where I launched my very successful *Auto Trader* magazine. However, at the time I didn't realize I would have to put it *all* back!

Having lost £20,000 a week when I took over in 1990, it has taken me 15 long years to get that up to £80,000 a week.

Sir Tom Finney, KBE

Known as the 'Preston Plumber', as he continued to mend pipes throughout his 14-year career with Preston, Bill Shankly once said of Sir Tom Finney: 'He would have been great in any team, in any match and in any age – even if he had been wearing an overcoat.'

Tommy Docherty and I played together at Preston back in the 1950s. Just after the end of the recent season we were both waiting in the corridor outside the chairman's office waiting to sign for the forthcoming season. In those days, you didn't have long-term contracts – you simply signed for each new term, and deals were always negotiated with the chairman. I was chatting with Tommy and asked him if he was going to sign. He said that he would if the terms were right. I went in, and the chairman said he would pay me twelve and ten. Twelve pounds during the playing season and ten pounds in the non-playing close season. I was happy with this and signed my name. I passed Tommy in the corridor and told him how it had gone. He nodded before heading into the chairman's office himself.

The chairman said to him, 'you've had a good season and played for Scotland haven't you, Tommy?'
'Yes I know,' came Tommy's reply, 'so what are the terms?'
'Twelve and eight' said the chairman immediately.
'I have just spoken to Finney outside and he said he's got twelve and ten,' exclaimed Tommy.
'I know' said the chairman, 'but he's a better player than you.'
'Not in the bloody close season he's not!' came the response.

Career Highlights

- *England international: 76 caps, 30 goals, 5th equal highest England goalscorer of all time*
- *In a career that spanned nearly a quarter of a century and over 600 senior games Sir Tom Finney was never booked*

Andy Cole

*Andy Cole was one of the most important Manchester United players of the last few decades.
His almost telepathic understanding with Dwight Yorke was a major force during the club's historic treble
season in 1999. He began his career at Arsenal, followed by spells at Fulham and Bristol City before
moving north to Newcastle at the tender age of 21. As the new young talent on Tyneside, he appeared to
have the world at his feet.*

If anybody asks what the price of fame is at Newcastle, there's only one notable answer: you
are transformed into a twenty-four-hour football chat line if you're lucky, and a jibbering
idiot if you are not.

Which brings me to the point where I almost assumed the latter role. It was a place called
Crook, a quiet, little mining village. And, arguably, trying to settle in there was the most
short-sighted mistake of my life so far. The place itself was OK, even if in my eyes it was like
something out of the dark ages. But, in truth, I was the one at fault, not the village or the very
nice people who occupied it. I was young, I was living alone, and I decided to rent a
five-bedroom house in the back of beyond. As daft as you can get, really. If I had been with
my family, it might well have been a sound arrangement. Cast as a bachelor boy, it was
madness. They rolled the pavements up in that place at nine o'clock and that was it.
It reminded me of things I watched on telly as a kid when they tried to portray a clichéd
version of living in the north. You know what I mean, all cobbled streets, smoking chimneys,
and stone terraces, a bit like the famous Hovis advert really. For me, it was all a bit too weird.
I landed in Crook merely because the manager suggested I would be much better with my
home on the south side of the City, making it far more convenient for the training ground
near Durham. It was in the countryside, as well, which had a certain appeal. There were four
shops in the village and mistakenly I thought I was getting away from it all. Peace and quiet,
switching off from the big, flash world of football, yeah, that's exactly what I decided
I wanted. But soon reality moved in and joined me. I started to get pestered with passers-by
banging on my front door every minute of the day. The rest of the time I was either in front
of the television or in a state of hibernation.

One night, Paul Stretford, then my newly acquired agent, popped round to discuss some
career details. When he arrived all he could see were the kids in the driveway almost swinging
from the guttering, and screaming through the letterbox for autographs. I was slumped in a
darkened living room, with both sets of curtains drawn and the television notched up to full
volume to drown out the palaver going on outside my front door. It felt as if I were a pop star,
and if that's what they have to deal with they are welcome to it. This all happened very quickly,
within a couple of weeks I would think, and Crook had taken on the proportions of the

continued...

Andy Cole

continued…

village of the damned. I had to get out. The city boy just couldn't take any more. Paul advised me to get my bags packed because we were leaving, and fast. He booked a suite at a hotel outside Durham, where my Newcastle teammate, Scott Sellars, another of his clients, was also staying. Then we headed off to discuss the accommodation arrangements with the club. Paul never revealed to me exactly what went on behind those locked doors but within a week I was relocated to a club apartment in an upmarket area of the city. It was a sensible move back to the place where I really belonged, a very nice place too, in a refurbished Victorian block with a great deal of privacy and security. I was now on the doorstep of the real action in the heart of Newcastle. It was a huge release for me. There, in an environment I related to far more easily, I was truly at home.

Career Highlights

⊛ *England international: 15 caps, 1 goal*

⊛ *5 Championships (1996, 1997, 1999, 2000 and 2001), 2 FA Cups (1996 and 1999) and a European Cup (1999) with Manchester United • League Cup (2002) with Blackburn*

Graeme Souness

Graeme Souness is known as one of football's hard men, a reputation formed during his glittering playing career with the dominant Liverpool side of the late 1970s and early 1980s. He has always done things his way: during his time in Glasgow he was banned from the touchline for a whole year, was subjected to death threats when he signed Mo Johnson – the first ever Roman Catholic to play for the Protestant club – and even found himself involved in suspicious car chases.

I bumped into a player one night in an Indian restaurant in Edinburgh. He was playing for another Scottish club and I casually asked him if he would be interested in joining Rangers the following season. It was not an illegal approach, more a case of two international colleagues having a chat over a meal and a glass of wine. He said he would like to come to Rangers but there was a small problem. He needed £30,000 in a hurry. He had a reputation as a gambler but I did not want to know what was going on in his private life. As this was a rather delicate situation I decided not to inform the chairman about the player's request and agreed to make him a personal loan without involving the club.

On the night I was due to meet the player with the cash, I dined with David Murray at Raffaelli's, and as we left the restaurant to get into his car, a motorbike with a long, thin number plate on the back drove by. It was a highly unusual sight, with the sharp edges protruding on either side of the machine. It was not something you see every day and it stuck in my mind. The chairman dropped me off at my apartment and an hour later I left carrying £30,000 in banknotes for my rendezvous at Tynecastle, which was only a matter of minutes away from where I lived.

As I drove away I noticed the same motorbike with the distinctive number plate at the end of my road. It was parked alongside a car and there was somebody sitting in the driver's seat. I was beginning to get suspicious and as I turned into the main road I was keeping an eye on my rear mirror. Sure enough the motorbike was behind me and 200 yards ahead was a set of traffic lights. I went through them on amber. I knew if he did not stop that I was being followed. He ignored the red light and stayed on my tail so I decided to take him on a bit of a wild-goose chase. Instead of heading for Tynecastle, I drove towards the area where I used to live. I know those streets like the back of my hand and I was on familiar territory. The bike stayed with me so I pulled into a garage to get petrol. The girl at the desk must have thought I was crazy because I had filled it up earlier in the day and now I was stopping to put a pound's worth into the tank.

Out of the corner of my eye I saw the motorcyclist drive past so when I got back inside the car I called my brother Bill on my mobile and told him I had a problem and asked him to meet me at my apartment as soon as he could. I reckoned there was one of two scenarios

continued...

Graeme Souness

continued...

unfolding here. Either the guy on the motorbike was checking that I was going to deliver the money or he was planning to take it off me. By now it must have been obvious to him that I was aware he was following me and when I reached my apartment my brother was waiting and the motorbike disappeared.

I did not want anything more to do with the player after that. To this day I have never asked him what it was all about but I would be curious to hear his side of it.

Career Highlights

⚽ *Scotland international: 54 caps, 4 goals*

⚽ *5 Championships (1979, 1980, 1982, 1983 and 1984), 4 League Cups (1981, 1982, 1983 and 1984) and 3 European Cups (1978, 1981 and 1984) with Liverpool • 3 Scottish Championships (1987, 1989 and 1990) and 4 Scottish League Cups (1987, 1988, 1990 and 1991) with Rangers (manager) • FA Cup (1992) with Liverpool (manager) • Turkish FA Cup (1996) with Galatasaray (manager) • League Cup (2002) with Blackburn (manager)*

Harry Redknapp

As a player Harry Redknapp turned out in the same West Ham team as Bobby Moore, Martin Peters and Geoff Hurst. As manager of the same club, he nurtured the considerable talents of Rio Ferdinand, Frank Lampard Jnr, Joe Cole and Michael Carrick. Harry's frank assessment of players and shrewd dealings in the transfer market have made him a firm favourite with the fans and media alike.

I'd watched Futre star for Portugal for many years and I was delighted when I got him to come to West Ham on a free transfer from AC Milan. Then Derby Manager Jim Smith was on the verge of signing him when I nipped in under his nose. Poor old Jim. I don't think he's ever forgiven me for it. One day I got a call from Jerome Anderson, the agent representing Futre in England, and he told me Futre was due to see Jim in Italy the following day. I couldn't believe it when he told me Futre was available on a free. 'He's had a bad injury,' he told me, 'but he's back playing again now.' I asked Jerome if he could arrange an interview with the Portuguese international and we fixed up a meeting at Heathrow Airport at 9 am the next morning. At the meeting I was instantly impressed. I could tell he wanted to play football, despite suffering an injury that had at one time threatened his career.

During our chat Futre's mobile phone rang. On the other end of the line was his Italian-based agent wondering where the hell Futre was. He had Jim Smith with him and they'd been searching high and low in Milan for the little Portuguese. Futre managed not to reveal his whereabouts and went on to complete a deal that suited both parties, with a very important clause: Futre agreed that if he was to suffer any further injuries we would cancel his contract with just a month's notice. His basic wage was good without being astronomical because most of his pay was based on appearances. I had struck a good deal. I drove him home feeling very pleased with myself, and grinned further when my wife, Sandra told me on the mobile during the journey that Jim Smith had been trying all day to contact me. Seconds later the mobile chirped into life again and it was Jim.

'Harry, where are you?'

'I'm in the car on the way home. Where are you?'

'I'm in Italy,' he said, as if I should have known. 'You haven't by any chance seen Paolo Futre, have you?'

'Who?' I asked, with just the right note of surprise in my voice. Olivier, eat your heart out.

'Paolo Futre,' he repeated. 'I've come to Italy to sign him and he ain't here. Someone said he was talking to you.'

Now I love Smithy, he is a good mate, so I couldn't lie to him any further. 'As it happens, Smithy, I've just met him at Heathrow Airport.'

'What?' he roared. 'You can't have. He's supposed to be here. We're all here to sign him.'

'Too late, Jim. He's just signed for West Ham.'

continued...

Harry Redknapp

continued...

The air went blue. He went berserk. You can just imagine that face getting redder and redder. 'Don't worry Jim,' I said. 'I'll send you a nice bottle of red wine,' and put the phone down with Smithy still effing and blinding.

Futre was a winner. He had suffered a bad knee injury and his best days were probably behind him but he wanted to play, wanted to train, and wanted to get fit. He'd captained Portugal, revelled in responsibility, and cared deeply about doing well for whatever club he played for. But all the time he carried his knee. You could tell it was always on his mind. For ten minutes he would do things you'd never seen in your life. He'd beat two or three players with an outrageous turn or feint, but he couldn't sustain it. You wouldn't see him for the next 20 minutes; he'd be stood still. I admired his attitude, although the story I'm about to recount should have made me question it.

It was the first League game of the 1996/97 season and we were up at Arsenal. I handed the team-sheet into the referee's room but when I got back to the dressing room Eddie Gillam, our trainer, told me he had a problem with Paolo and the shirts.

'What kind of problem,' I asked, innocently. 'Doesn't it fit him?'

But it was a lot more serious than that. We'd allocated number 16 to Futre, but he thought such a shirt was an insult.

'Futre,' he said, pointing to his chest 'Futre number 10.'

I explained to him that he had to wear number 16, that it wasn't like the old days when players could wear different numbers every week, that it was FA rules that players were allocated a squad number at the beginning of the season and were stuck with it. But I may as well have recited a nursery rhyme. 'Futre,' he shouted, jabbing his chest again. 'Futre. Eusebio number 10. Futre number 10.'

'Yeah I understand all that,' I said, 'but there's nothing we can do. Moncur is number 10. You are number 16. We can't change it now.'
'No f★★★★★g way 16,' Futre said, his voice rising further.
'F★★★★★g number 10.'
By this stage there were only about 45 minutes to the kick-off, the sun was shining, and thousands of fans at Highbury were looking forward excitedly to the new season.
'Look,' I said. 'Just wear the number 16 shirt and go out and play. We'll talk about it later.'

continued...

Harry Redknapp

continued...

But he wouldn't have it. By this time the commotion had attracted the attention of the other players and they all looked to see what was going on, while pretending to prepare for the match.

'Okay then,' I said. 'What are you going to do?'

'F★★★ off,' he said. 'No play.'

I'd heard enough. I used Futre's colourful expressions to tell him where to go and next minute he was off, in a cab and home.

Career Highlights

⊛   Division One title (2003) with Portsmouth (manager)

⊛   Inter-Toto Cup (1999) with West Ham United (manager)

Jose Mourinho

After a modest playing career, Jose Mourinho completed a UEFA coaching course while still in his twenties. He took his first management job at Benfica, before a stint at Uniao de Leiria followed by a remarkable two years at Porto. His achievements in Portugal saw him appointed manager of Chelsea in 2004, where his methodical and clinical approach brought immediate success.

My first game as a manager, at Benfica, was against Boavista in September 2000. Obviously I asked the club's observation department to prepare a detailed report on the opposition in the days leading to the game, this is normal. But when the report arrived I found a team made up of only 10 players. I could not believe it, and not only that, the player they left out was Sanchez, one of Boavista's most influential players. Of course I never asked them to do another report for me.

Career Highlights

⊛   *2 Portuguese Championships (2003 and 2004), Portuguese Cup (2003), UEFA Cup (2003) and a European Cup (2004) with Porto (manager)* • *Championship (2005) and League Cup (2005) with Chelsea (manager)*

Barry Fry

Barry Fry is undoubtedly one of the most colourful characters English football has ever seen. His managerial career started in front of 37 paying spectators at Dunstable Town in 1974, and during his lengthy involvement in the game, he has changed the fortunes of a number of struggling clubs. At Barnet FC, he typically did everything in his power to keep the club afloat.

My wife Kristine is a strange sort of breed, with a German mother and a Scottish father. I had to fight the German and Scottish armies together to get her, but she was worth it. The German tradition is to have what we would call Christmas Day on Christmas Eve and we travelled to Bedford from Dunstable to have dinner with them. When we got home at midnight, there was more than a touch of frost in the air. Our Boxing Day fixture was a home match against Wealdstone, with an 11am kick off. Once again the lads had had no money for four weeks, but it was more serious this time because of the season of the year. I said to Kristine: 'We've got to make sure the match is on. I'm going to the club to roll the pitch.' She looked at me aghast but said: 'I'll come with you.' So we headed for Barnet.

She goes into the office and puts the kettle on while I go into the corner of the ground, get a tractor out and affix the roller to the back of it and drive it onto the playing area. It's now one o'clock on Christmas morning and pitch black. I'm going up and down like a good'un, whistling and singing away, and I give her a wave as I near the clubhouse. I turn the tractor, with its two lights at the front, to roll the next patch of ground and as I do so, I see all these coppers jumping over the fence, shining their torches and making their way towards me. I slowed down as I approached them.

'Yeah?'

'Get off that tractor!' yelled one of them. 'We are arresting you for being drunk and disorderly.'

'F**k off, I'm the manager of Barnet Football Club.'

'Yeah, sure, and I'm George Best. Get off the tractor! All the neighbours around here have been complaining about this drunkard singing Christmas carols in the early hours of the morning. You are under arrest.'

I shut the tractor down and jumped off. The local policeman arrived at the scene of the crime in the nick of time, shone a torch in my face and fortunately identified me to his colleagues.

continued...

Barry Fry

continued...

'Baz,' he said, 'we've got to stop you. We've had so many complaints. There are kids sleeping. It's Christmas morning for Christ's sake.'

Before I was rudely interrupted I had managed to roll only half the pitch. This looked terrific, all neatly packed so that the ball would just bounce off it, but when I arrived at the ground on Boxing Day the other half was such a mess that the referee called off the game. It broke my heart.

Career Highlights

⊕   *Taking Barnet from the Vauxhall Conference to Division 2 between 1986 and 1993*

⊕   *Barry describes saving Southend from almost certain relegation to Division 2 as his single greatest achievement*

Andy Gray

Andy Gray has played a pivotal role in the development of Sky Sports' football coverage. His contribution has been widely recognized with a number of awards including the Royal Television Society's Sports Presenter of the Year. As a player, he became the only footballer to win the PFA Player of the Year and Young Player of the Year in the same season (1977).

The Wolverhampton folk or the Black Country people have a very dry sense of humour which is best illustrated by a wonderful story of when Villa chief scout, Don Dorman, went to sign a promising young lad. Don had been watching this strapping young lad for some time and when he called at the family's home found they were all big and built like mountains. There were three boys all over six foot tall and about as wide, while dad was even bigger and mum too was a well-built, handsome lady. So Don politely asks the father what the secret of having such a strong healthy family is. 'Stew,' says the dad. 'Mother's speciality is home made stew. It's grand stuff and will make a man of anyone.' They then went off to the local pub to have a drink and a chat about the lad signing as a professional footballer. Don is invited back to the house eventually, for a plate of mum's legendary stew as the pot is always on the boil. And sure enough the stew is the best he's ever tasted. On the way out Don happens to see the family's pet bull mastiff lying in front of the fire and can't ignore the fact the animal is better endowed than any other he's ever seen. He asks the dad about it and jokes whether the dog eats the stew as well. Dad answers in his thick Black Country accent: 'No, it's amazing really, he only licks the plates!'

Career Highlights

⚽ *Scotland international: 20 caps, 7 goals*

⚽ *Championship (1985), FA Cup (1984) and a European Cup Winners' Cup (1985) with Everton*

● *Scottish Championship (1989) with Rangers*

Viv Anderson, MBE

Viv Anderson was the first black player to appear in a full international for England. However, this classy defender deserves to be remembered for more than just that. During a long and impressive career with some of England's top clubs, he won everything the domestic game had to offer. It all started at Nottingham Forest under the mercurial Brian Clough back in 1972.

As a young apprentice at Forest, I was doing my chores in the boot room one afternoon when the phone rang. I guessed it would be Brian Clough, one of the most terrifying men that any teenage apprentice could ever hope to serve under. Another one of the apprentices at the time picked it up and said, 'hello?' Sure enough, it was the manager.

'Young man, I want three teas in my office.'

'Get them yourself,' came the response from a very brave apprentice.

A pause.

'Do you know who you're speaking to?' asked the presumably gobsmacked manager.

'Yeah.'

'I want three teas in my office,' he barked a second time.

'Get them yourself,' replied the apprentice again.

'Are you sure you know who you're talking to kid?' asked Cloughie in astonishment.

'Yup,' replied the apprentice, before putting the phone down and carrying on as if nothing had happened.

Anyone who knows what sort of man Brian Clough was will appreciate quite how brave – or even stupid – the apprentice was being during this encounter. I can only speculate as to what Cloughie was thinking at the other end of that phone, but all I know is that no effort was made to identify the lad and the incident was never mentioned again. Just maybe the unthinkable had happened, and Brian Clough had been stunned into silence.

Career Highlights

⚽ *England international: 30 caps, 2 goals*

⚽ *Championship (1978), 2 League Cups (1978 and 1979) and 2 European Cups (1979 and 1980) with Nottingham Forest • League Cup (1987) with Arsenal • FA Cup (1990) with Manchester United*

John Toshack, MBE

Two-time Welsh manager John Toshack started his footballing career with Cardiff City, signing for them as a 17-year-old. Despite his strong affection for Cardiff, after four years at Ninian Park he was signed by Liverpool in November 1970. During his time at Anfield, John was part of a very special era in the Reds' history but never forgot his roots in Wales.

It was always nice to go back and play at Ninian Park, and in my Liverpool days I always received a warm welcome from the home crowd on international days. When I left Cardiff they were top of Division Two, and the season just ended had seen them gain promotion from Division Three – back to the status that they had held for so long. I mention this because of a lovely story that can be told concerning a lifelong Cardiff City supporter.

At every football club there is someone who has seen it all from year dot, usually an old-age pensioner who works voluntarily at the ground cleaning toilets, sweeping terraces, doing anything just to feel a part of 'his' club. At Liverpool the man concerned was called Henry and he would do all the little things that can go unnoticed around the dressing-room area. Shampoos for the players, newspapers, regular trips to the chemist or the cobblers, all the little tasks that need doing from time to time. At Swansea the name of the man is Haydn. An incredible fellow, always telling the lads jokes, he walks around using a tie for a belt and can be seen every Sunday morning cleaning the seats in the centre stand. Both Henry and Haydn are seventy-odd, and their counter-part at Cardiff, Ted Harris, would be about the same age now. As I walked into Ninian Park for the Yugoslavia game I was feeling very proud after a season that had seen me pick up two winners' medals at Anfield. The League Championship had been sewn up ten days earlier, and in my pocket was the UEFA Cup medal I had won two days before in Belgium. I had travelled to Cardiff straight from Brussels airport, and when I got to the ground with the Welsh team the first person I bumped into was Ted Harris.

'Hello Ted, how are you?' Then Ted blurted out one of the best lines I have heard in my many years in the game:
'See the City's gone up, ay, bet you wish you was here now, don't you?'

continued...

John Toshack, MBE

continued...

I don't think Ted realized that they were top of Division Two when I left, or that I had won two medals that season with the best club in Europe! I certainly wasn't going to spoil things and remind him, so I just said 'You're bloody right, Ted, I do.' I can imagine him going off and telling all his mates that John Toshack told him he would prefer to be at Cardiff than at Liverpool! Haydn, Henry and Ted – they are not well known in the football media, but believe me, they are what the game is all about.

Career Highlights

⚽ *Wales international: 40 caps, 13 goals, Wales manager (1994 and 2004-Present)*

⚽ *3 Championships (1973, 1976 and 1977), FA Cup (1974) and 2 UEFA Cups (1973 and 1976) with Liverpool • Spanish Championship (1990) with Real Madrid (manager)*

Mohamed Al Fayed

When the Harrods' owner took over as Fulham chairman on May 29th 1997 it was undoubtedly the single most significant moment in the club's history. Over the following years, Fulham FC was able to establish itself in the Premiership.

I have been involved in football most of my life. As a boy growing up in Egypt I organized my own team made up of my brothers and our school friends to play matches in our home city of Alexandria.

At that time we were all passionate fans of the English clubs whose exploits we listened to every week on the BBC World Service commentaries. It was through those crackly static-filled broadcasts that I first heard of Fulham and decided to make it my favourite team.

When I came to live and work in Britain many years later it was naturally Craven Cottage that I went to stand on the terraces at that romantic riverside ground and support the fortune of 'The Whites'.

Perhaps the most interesting experience I've ever had in football, though, was the day I invited Michael Jackson to be my guest at Craven Cottage.

It was in April 1999 when Fulham, under the management of Kevin Keegan, were poised to gain promotion from the Second to the First Division and a victory at home to Wigan would virtually clinch the championship.

Michael Jackson, whom I had known for several years, had flown in that day from New York and came to visit me at Harrods where he wanted to do some shopping. I was going on to the match that afternoon so I asked Michael to come along too. I knew it would be a surprise and a great thrill to the Fulham fans to see the King of Pop in person.

I pulled his leg about the heavy make-up he was wearing as being inappropriate for a football spectator, but it was, after all, part of his well-known public image and he took my jokes in good heart.

I have received such warm affection from the Fulham fans since I saved the club from extinction that it has become my practice to walk around the pitch before every home match so that I can wave to the crowd and thank them for their support.

continued...

Mohamed Al Fayed

continued...

On this particular afternoon, when our master of ceremonies, David Hamilton, announced that I would be accompanied by Michael Jackson there were gasps of amazement all round the ground. The supporters didn't quite believe that it was the real Michael Jackson. They thought I had produced a look-alike.

But Michael was great. He walked around the pitch wearing a Fulham scarf, carrying a Fulham umbrella, and even giving an impromptu performance of his trademark Moonwalk.

When it came to the actual football, however, it was difficult to maintain his interest. The tricky bit was when I tried to explain the offside rule to him. Football fans, of course, understand offside almost instinctively but try getting it across to someone who has never watched the game before. Michael is not into sport and added to that he is an American. As we all know, the Americans treat soccer as a minority sport behind baseball, basketball, American football and ice hockey. Michael was very polite but I could tell that he didn't understand a word I was saying.

After the game I took him into the dressing room to meet the players. I always have a laugh and a joke with my players so before I entered with Michael I shouted to them something about covering 'themselves' up. The players roared with laughter and Michael grinned but I'm not sure that he saw the funny side. All he said was: 'Good game, lads.'

On a tour of Craven Cottage the only thing which really interested him was a set of old black and white photographs from the 1920s which showed players wearing trilby hats like the one he was wearing on that day.

As he left he told the press: 'I loved it. I'm looking forward to coming again.'

Another new Fulham fan had been created that bizarre day.

Incidentally Fulham won the match 2–0 and went on to gain promotion.

Stuart McCall

Glasgow Rangers great Stuart McCall is an Ibrox hero, but the other club in his life has been Bradford City. A product of City's youth system, Stuart made his debut at Reading on 28 August 1982 having served a good old-fashioned apprenticeship.

I made my mark on Bradford City pretty quickly as an apprentice. Well, I put the 'Welcome to Valley Parade' sign up on the outside of the ground as one of my jobs. It was a hard working day, starting early and doing all the run around stuff. There were only three of us at the time because that's all the club could afford. John Hanson and Carl Leneghan were the other two. We were groundsmen – I had to put the divots back at the end of games – painters of the crush barriers, cleaners of the bath, it was your life. I was also the boot boy and had 32 pairs to do; shining them up and even making the soles gleam for the players I liked who looked after me. The youngsters today don't know they are born. Scrubbing floors and pulling the hairs out of the bath, they don't realise what life was like in those days for a young hopeful like me.

Obviously I was keen to impress, so on the first day Brian Edwards asked me to go to the chemist and get him a couple of plasters. Before I went I heard this hoarse Irish voice behind me. I had been told about this guy and to look out when he was about. It was Bobby Campbell. I thought I would impress him and told him I was going up to the chemist, so did he want some lozenges for his throat? In two seconds he had me up against the wall by the throat with my legs dangling and let me know in his own style that he always talked like that. Here was me trying to be a nice boy and a credit to the community and that was my reward. I was trembling for hours after. Bobby was not a man to cross. Mind you he did let me get him some Anadin for his hangover when I was at the shops.

Although the jobs were difficult as an apprentice I was thrown in with the first-team players to train. I mixed with good pros with good habits and great crack and I was eager to learn from them. People like David McNiven and Mick Bates had played at a higher level with Leeds, while Terry Dolan had been at Arsenal. Bobby Campbell was the main man. Other guys like Ces Pod, Les Chapman and Gary Watson were really helpful. I was their slave from the start of the day to the finish. If anything wasn't right, like a pair of socks missing, I would get it in the neck. We had a Scottish coach, Lammie Robertson, who was good to me. We shared the same passion for Scotland and he looked out for me.

continued...

Stuart McCall

continued...

But even your friends like a wind up and I fell for one famously. Lammie told me that Brian Edwards wanted me to go out in my lunch hour to Madeley's DIY store down the hill and ask the manager for a 'long weight' he needed for some work he was doing on the gym. Now normally I would also get the pies during lunch and bring them back for the rest of the lads, but like a good apprentice I went into the store first and said I have been sent down for a 'long weight' and could they give me one. The boy on the checkout went into the back office and another assistant came. 'Are you from Bradford City? Oh, you're the one who wants a long weight. We'll give you one all right.' Half an hour passed and no one came out, I was panicking because I thought the boys would be missing their lunch because of me. An hour was nearly up when the assistant came out again. 'There you are,' he said. 'You've had a really long wait now.' It dawned on me. I felt two inches tall and my face went bright red!

Career Highlights

⚽ *Scotland international: 40 caps, 1 goal*

⚽ *6 Championships (1992, 1993, 1994, 1995, 1996 and 1997), 3 Scottish Cups (1992, 1993 and 1996)*
  and 3 Scottish League Cups (1992, 1993 and 1996) with Rangers

Roy Keane

Roy Keane has been a giant of the British game for over a decade. When one considers that he has played under three of the best managers the game has known – Brian Clough, Sir Alex Ferguson and Jack Charlton – it shouldn't come as a surprise that he has achieved so much.

In my heart of hearts I knew I could never refuse to sign for the world's most famous football club – Manchester United.

When I flew to Manchester, Alex Ferguson met me at the airport. We drove to his home close by and Brian Kidd was also there. After a meal and some general chat, Ferguson suggested we have a game of snooker. He was a useful player. I wasn't bad myself. Manchester United, the Premier League Champions wanted to buy me. I thought it prudent to let him win.

Career Highlights

- *Republic of Ireland international: 63 caps, 9 goals*

- *7 Championships (1994, 1996, 1997, 1999, 2000, 2001, 2003), 4 FA Cups (1994, 1996, 1999, 2004), League Cup (1994) and a European Cup (1999) with Manchester United*

Dennis Bergkamp

The Dutch maestro has won and learnt much under the guidance of the philosophical Arsène Wenger.

Behind every kick of a ball, there has to be a thought.

Career Highlights

⚽ *Holland international: 79 caps, 37 goals*

⚽ *Dutch Championship (1990), 3 Dutch FA Cups (1986, 1987 and 1993), European Cup Winners' Cup (1987) and UEFA Cup (1992) with Ajax • UEFA Cup (1994) with Inter Milan • 3 Championships (1998, 2002 and 2004) and 3 FA Cups (1998, 2002 and 2003) with Arsenal*

Jimmy Hill, OBE

As chairman of the PFA (1957–61), Jimmy Hill led the successful campaign to lift the £20 maximum wage. As chairman of Fulham, whom he served so well as a player, he managed to steer them away from a merger with Queen's Park Rangers and successfully lead them through a critical period in their history.

At Fulham FC, I was fortunate to play with Charlie Mitten. He was a really extraordinary character and, in his day, a controversial name in the football world. His contract with Manchester United had expired when he went on a summer tour with them to the USA in 1950, but instead of signing an extension with United he ended up signing for Colombian club Santa Fé. In those days moving abroad was a bizarre thing to do, particularly given that Colombia were expelled from FIFA at the time.

When Colombia rejoined FIFA the following year, Charlie was forced to return to Manchester United where he was immediately transfer listed and sold to Fulham, and it was here that I got to know him. His great passion was greyhound racing and he had his own dog, although it wasn't until I was having a spell of injury that I learnt this fact under the most unusual circumstances.

We usually trained in the mornings, but I would return in the afternoons to receive treatment on my injury from the Fulham physio Frank Penn. One such afternoon I arrived for my usual appointment at 2.00 pm, but as I hobbled into the treatment room, was stunned to discover a greyhound lying stretched out on the treatment table, as a straightfaced Frank Penn worked delicately and carefully on its lean muscles. In the corner Charlie Mitten was looking on intently. He hardly batted an eyelid as I limped into the room, and calmly explained that the dog had a big race coming up and was nursing a slight strain. So there I stood, a top-flight professional footballer, gingerly supporting myself on my one good leg, patiently waiting for Charlie Mitten's dog to finish his massage. It would never happen at a football club now of course, but Charlie Mitten was a law unto himself and had the nerve to do just about anything – and pull it off.

Career Highlights

⚽ *Took Coventry from Division 3 to Division 1 in five seasons (1961–1966)*

⚽ *Making over 600 appearances as the front man for Match of the Day*

⚽ *Pioneering the 3-points for a win system introduced by the Football Association in 1981*

Team Life

Alan Shearer, OBE

Alan Shearer has been one of the most feared and respected strikers of the modern era and a wonderful ambassador for the game. Despite his remarkable scoring record for club and country, he has only won one major trophy – a League Championship with Blackburn, and it was at Ewood Park that he made one of his lifelong friendships.

When I first joined Blackburn, we went straight off to Scotland for a pre-season trip and I hit it off with Mike Newell straightaway. When we returned he invited me for a round of golf at Southport and I soon fell in love with the area. Mike suggested that I had a look at a rented house in Formby, which had once been occupied by Everton midfielder Kevin Sheedy, and that is where I lived before my wife and I bought our own house.

Before Lainya moved up from Southampton, I spent a lot of time at the Newells' home and they played a big part in helping me to settle in. Eventually Mike and I became near neighbours, regular golf partners and daily travelling companions on the journey to the Blackburn training ground. Mike is the sort of bloke who loves an argument. He is known everywhere as Mr. Angry. He will argue black is white, even if all the facts are loaded against him.

Eventually, when Tim Flowers joined Blackburn from Southampton, he also moved into the same area and the three of us shared a car to training each day. The favourite pastime on the fifty-minute trip was winding up Mike. I would catch Tim's eye in the rear-view mirror and give him a little wink. We would pick on certain players who we knew Mike didn't rate and start singing their praises. Mike would bite every time. He would rant and rave and the two of us would struggle to keep straight faces.

Once, after dropping Tim off at his house, I gave him a little hoot on my car horn and that led to an hour's argument between Mike and myself about the times of the day you could use your horn. Often we would part company in a rage but next day it was as if nothing had happened. It was all rather childish but in Mike and Tim I know I have made two friends for life.

Career Highlights

⚽ *England international: 63 caps, 30 goals, 5th equal highest England goalscorer of all time*

⚽ *Championship (1995) with Blackburn*

Jim Smith

Jim Smith is one of football's most enduring and well-liked personalities. Highlights of the 'Bald Eagle's' career include his days at the Manor Ground when Oxford were crowned champions in successive seasons as they stormed their way out of the old Third Division into the top flight. During his playing days he played for Sheffield United, Aldershot, Halifax Town and Lincoln City. At Halifax Town he played under Alan Ball Sr. and the unwittingly entertaining Harry Hubbick.

When Alan Ball Sr. started out as manager of Halifax, it was with this amazing intensity, but it gradually tailed off and he started missing training. He would arrive at lunchtime and say we were not working hard enough and make us report back in the afternoon to suit his timetable. Often, he left the training to his right hand man Harry Hubbick, a remarkable character.

He had played for Bolton Wanderers when they were Bolton Wanderers and they say Stanley Matthews never got a kick against him – or at least, Stanley got a few kicks, but they weren't of the ball.

Harry was not the brightest of men – at training he would say: 'Fifty per cent go with him; fifty per cent go with him; and the other fifty per cent come with me.'

When Ball started missing training, we would tell Harry to go easy on us. He would say: 'OK, but when you go past the manager's office, breathe heavy!' Harry would have us doing sprints and would shout: 'On your marks ... go!' but would forget which hand he had the whistle in and stick his finger in his mouth and blow.

I remember him once driving from the training ground to Halifax's Shay stadium with a few of the lads in his car. He had to turn right to enter the ground, but did not indicate and an overtaking car smashed into the side of him. A furious Harry got out and bellowed at the driver: 'you daft bugger, you could see I was turning into the ground, I've got my track suit on!'

On another occasion we had a mock tribunal for Tony Field, who had been sent off, and the verdict was a £25 fine and 28 days. 'Wait a minute,' said Harry, 'Shouldn't we give him a £25 fine and a month!' And he was serious.

There were certainly a few laughs at Halifax!

Career Highlights

⚽ Promotions with Colchester (1974 – Division 4 to Division 3), Birmingham (1980 – Division 2 to Division 1), Oxford (1984 and 1985 – Division 3 to Division 1) and Derby (1995 – Division 1 to the Premiership)

Joe Royle

As a manager Joe Royle won the FA Cup with Everton and secured promotion with both Oldham and Manchester City. The amiable Merseysider began his playing career at Everton where he made over 270 appearances and scored 119 goals, including 23 in the 1970 Championship winning side.

When I was a young pro at Everton, there was another player in the squad called Sandy Brown. In those days a lot of footballers used talcum powder, and Sandy used it after training every day without fail. During one afternoon session, one of the lads quietly slipped into the dressing room and, having emptied out the entire contents of Sandy's precious talcum powder bottle, replaced it with tiling grout. A little while later we all trotted in from the training ground and headed for the showers as usual. As we watched out of the corners of our eyes, Sandy stepped out of the shower and, while still a little damp, started liberally covering himself in what he thought was his talcum powder. Our sly glances turned to open ridicule as, to his horror and surprise, his body quickly set into a mound of chunky, gluey paste. The whole team rolled about in hysterics, but it took poor Sandy a little while before he found the funny side of it all.

Career Highlights

- *England international: 6 caps, 2 goals*
- *Championship (1970) with Everton • League Cup (1976) with Manchester City • FA Cup (1995) with Everton (manager)*

Luther Blissett

Luther Blissett was a crucial part of the Graham Taylor-led Watford side that rose up through the lower ranks of English football to eventually finish second behind Liverpool in the 1982–83 Championship race. His form during this season saw him rewarded with a place in Sir Bobby Robson's England squad and a summer move to Italian giants AC Milan for a brief spell before returning to Watford.

At the time of this story, Watford were in the third division. The season had been going pretty well – we were in second place – but the pressure was on and some indifferent performances had taken their toll on squad morale.

Following yet another poor weekend's display, and an equally dismal training session on the Monday, the manager Graham Taylor called a team meeting in the middle of the pitch, with him and his two coaches, John Ward and Steve Harrison.

He announced, in no uncertain terms, that we were training and playing as if we had lumps of concrete on our shoulders, and he was absolutely right: what we needed was to get back to enjoying our football again. But despite the manager's pep talk, the mood at training remained really low for the next couple of days, and progress was almost non-existent.

It was clear that something pretty drastic was needed to shake us out of this rut, and on the Thursday in the changing room before what we were sure would be another miserable training session, in walked Steve Harrison and John Ward carrying two big bags. We looked on amazed as they tipped out a huge haul of gear they'd raided from a local fancy dress shop and told us to put it on.

Picture the scene: it's a damp, cold, grey morning in March, and 25 burly and intense professional footballers are running purposefully out onto the field for a crucial, season-defining training session decked out in pirate's eye patches, fake moustaches, big rubber noses and clown wigs.

The idea was inspired: the way to lift the blanket of depression that was holding us back was simply to start enjoying training and playing again. It was a great session and we were soon back to our winning ways – at the end of the season Watford were promoted.

Career Highlights

- England international: 14 caps, 3 goals
- Promotion to the Third Division (1978), Second Division (1979) and First Division (1982) with Watford

Pat Rice

Pat Rice has played a part in all three of Arsenals 'doubles', either as player or coach. He played in the 1971 side and was Arsène Wenger's assistant as the club won the 'double' for the second time 27 years later, and again in 2002.

I recently received an award from the Arsenal chairman Peter Hill-Wood for 40 years of service at the club. As he gave me the award he said that all those years ago when he first saw me playing as an amateur in the Arsenal youth team he made quite a point of telling everyone at the London Colney training ground that there was absolutely no way I would ever make it as a player. He said soon after that, he made a mental note never to comment on a player's potential again!

Career Highlights

⊕ *Northern Ireland international: 49 caps*

⊕ *Championship (1971) and 2 FA Cups (1971 and 1979) with Arsenal*

Mark Bright

In an 18-year career, Mark Bright played for Leicester, Crystal Palace, Sheffield Wednesday and Millwall, before ending his playing days at Charlton. He scored 209 goals in 574 games. The high point of Mark's football career was probably his prolific striking partnership at Palace with Ian Wright during the late 1980s and early 1990s – a high-achieving era that he decided to remind his Charlton teammates of in an unusual fashion.

When I was at Charlton Athletic the boys would vote every Friday morning for the player who had been the worst trainer of the week. The chosen player would then have to do the Friday session in a bright yellow shirt with the words 'I've had a Brightmare' printed on the back – a reference to the fact that I had worn it so many times. One week I decided to get my own back for this ribbing, and took the shirt away to have some alterations made. Predictably that Friday they all voted for me and, as I stepped forward to collect the yellow shirt from the assistant manager Keith Peacock, he unfolded it so everyone could see the back, which now read: '2 FA Cup finals, 1 League Cup final, 1 Golden Boot, 200 goals, 2 promotions – not bad for a Brightmare!'

Needless to say the players loved it.

Career Highlights

❂ *FA Cup runner-up (1990) with Crystal Palace • FA Cup runner-up (1993) and League Cup runner-up (1993) with Sheffield Wednesday*

Dave Bassett

Affectionately known as 'Harry', Dave Bassett is one of the most experienced managers in the game. He is probably best known for guiding his unfashionable Wimbledon side to the First Division in the 1980s. Bassett formed the original 'Crazy Gang', and life at Plough Lane was never dull.

After relegation to the Fourth Division in the summer of 1982, we were joined by a new club physiotherapist, Derek French, a man who was born to be part of the crazy, zany, almost surrealistic rise of Wimbledon over the next four years.

When I found him, Derek was dividing his life between working as a part-time physio at Barnet and driving a mini-cab. We were certainly no wealthier than Barnet and when 'Frenchie', as he was always known to us, came to us, we told him not to give up his mini-cabbing.

He was the club fall guy and the butt of several cruel jokes – but he took most of them well. He wasn't too impressed, though, when Wally Downes almost drowned him during the club's first pre-season tour of Finland. All the boys had gone for a swim in the lake and it seemed quite important to Wally that he should discover just how long Frenchie could survive under water. He went to the limit.

On a later occasion, a couple of the younger members of the team dangled him over the side of a boat by his ankles in a Finnish port. There was a heavy swell and Frenchie was screaming for his life as money and personal belongings cascaded from his pockets into the murky sea before they eventually hauled him back to safety. He will also claim that Mark Morris, quite wilfully, attempted to decapitate him during pre-season training. I was illustrating a tactical point from a free-kick position and had used Frenchie as part of the defensive 'wall'. On the word 'go', he was to take off like a rocket and charge the ball. He did exactly that but, as he charged forward, Morris' arm shot out and karate-chopped him straight across the windpipe.

Frenchie also dines out on the tale of the League match during which he rushed on to the pitch to attend a minor injury. Wally Downes – who else? – thought he looked a bit hot and so picked up the bucket and emptied it over Frenchie's head, much to the surprise and delight of the crowd. Frenchie has only been close to committing murder on one occasion. He had injured his foot during a training incident and one of the players, Steve Galliers, at first showing a great deal of mock concern over the injury, suddenly jumped on it. Frenchie's scream of agony must have been heard throughout South London. Everyone who had witnessed the incident has an abiding memory of our revered physio hobbling after a somewhat fitter Mr. Galliers, screaming: 'I'll kill you, you b*****d, I'll kill you.'

continued...

Dave Bassett

continued...

Fortunately, I've always been in favour of high spirits and, with a bunch like Wimbledon's Crazy Gang, the worst thing that I could have done would have been to interfere, or take any form of disciplinary action. As far as I am concerned, players who work hard are entitled to play hard – but every one of them knows the penalty if they allow that play time to affect their performance on the pitch.

Career Highlights

⚽ *Wimbledon were elected to the Football League in 1977. Dave Bassett helped lift the Dons from Division Four to Division One in just four seasons during the 1980s*

⚽ *Taken clubs to promotion 8 times: Wimbledon (4 times), Sheffield United (twice), Crystal Palace (once) and Nottingham Forest (once)*

Peter Shilton, CBE

Peter Shilton is England's most capped player ever, turning out an astonishing 125 times and conceding only 80 goals. He is also England's oldest ever captain, leading the team out at the age of 40 for the Third Place play-off vs. Italy in 1990. His domestic career was equally impressive, winning a handful of medals, most of which came during his successful stint in the Nottingham Forest goal.

When I was a player at Nottingham Forest, we played Barcelona in the European Super Cup. In those days it was a two-leg affair, and the first leg was in Nottingham at the City Ground on 30th of January 1980. In the mornings, the day before a home game, we always used to leave the stadium and jog along the river Trent to our training ground. We didn't have the greatest facilities, and certainly nothing like the lush training grounds that exist these days. We had a reasonable pitch to practise on, but everywhere else was wild grassland with lots of bracken, weeds and thorns. Brian Clough, one the game's toughest taskmasters, used to send us all off for gruelling runs through the undergrowth to make sure that we kept our feet firmly on the ground and didn't get too big headed. We all used to be appalled when he suggested these runs, but it was his way of showing us who was boss and it worked.

Having finished a particularly punishing run on the eve of the Barcelona game, we were making our way back up the canal to the stadium – panting and looking like we'd picked a fight with a hedge and lost – when the luxurious Barcelona coach pulled up to the training ground alongside us. The Spaniards stepped grandly off the coach in their brand new, top of the range shiny red and blue training suits to be greeted by our lot – bloodied, bruised and battered, with brambles in our hair, rips in our socks and manic but determined grimaces on our faces. I don't think they could believe their eyes! They took one look at us and our rugged training facilities before hopping straight back onto their coach again. As they drove off, we all stood laughing like mad and thinking to ourselves – we've got this soft lot beat already! And we did, winning at home and drawing away.

Career Highlights

- *England international: 125 caps, England's most capped international*
- *Championship (1978), 2 League Cups (1978 and 1979) and 2 European Cups (1979 and 1980) with Nottingham Forest • Peter Shilton made a record 1,005 appearances during his career*

Alan Curbishley

One of the country's most talented coaches, Alan Curbishley has worked wonders during his time at Charlton Athletic. Despite the tight financial constraints, he has turned the Addicks into an established Premiership team.

A very young and nervous Scott Parker joined in the conversation at the back of the coach after an away victory. Scott had just broken into the first team and was keen to be a part of it. The talk was about food and restaurants, with each player taking it in turn to mention their favourite meal, etc. When Scott excitedly joined in saying 'I really like Chinese,' someone asked him what his favourite Chinese dish was.

'Well I really like that *animated duck*, it's great,' he said.

All the lads rolled up, not only had Scott become a first team player he also learned very early to make sure he thought before he spoke!

Career Highlights

* Curbishley has turned a struggling first division side into an entertaining, mid-table Premiership outfit – an achievement that cannot be underestimated. Charlton manager 1991–present

Alan Ball, MBE

A World Cup winner at 21, Alan Ball was the youngest member of the victorious 1966 England team. However, the campaign in Mexico four years later was to end in disappointment.

After we had just lost in the quarter-final to West Germany, we went back to our hotel somehow hoping to wake up from the nightmare. I am not sure if the disappointment has ever eased but back at the hotel, with a few beers on the lawn beside the pool, we had a bit of a wake that produced a false charge of cheerfulness. Three of the lads and their wives had gone straight off to Acapulco immediately. I could not have done that but had to be part of the whole experience until we left the plane at Heathrow.

There was an amusing moment the following morning on the long coach trip from León to Mexico City. Tommy Wright lapsed into tears, and as he was crying Sir Alf Ramsey came up to him and put a sympathetic, fatherly arm around him, saying: 'Don't be too upset, young man. You've got plenty of time. There's another World Cup coming up in four years' time and you're young enough to be in that.'

There was a pause, and then Tommy delivered his reply and his reason for being upset. 'There's no beer left on the bus,' he said.

Career Highlights

⊕ *England international: 72 caps, 8 goals*

⊕ *World Cup (1966)* • *Championship (1970) with Everton*

Glenn Hoddle

Glenn Hoddle is regarded by some as Tottenham's greatest ever player, having won FA Cup and UEFA Cup honours with the north London side, making some 500 appearances between 1975 and 1987. He is also an England legend, taking part in World Cups as both player and manager. Perhaps his greatest night in the latter capacity was the heroic, blood-stained 0-0 draw in Rome that took England to the 1998 World Cup in France.

Supporters often wonder what it's like on board a team bus bound for a game. Well, that night it was surprisingly quiet. There were the usual card schools, a bit of banter about the music playing, but mostly a lot of silence. You couldn't help but notice the most splendid Roman sunset as we approached the city, and it was at this moment that I sensed it might be a glorious night.

Both John Gorman and I dropped off, but only briefly. We'd specially prepared two videos to play on the coach. One reminded the players of the great England footballing tradition they were following – World Cup '66, Euro '96, and legendary players like Bobby Moore, Gordon Banks, Bobby Charlton and Geoff Hurst. The other reminded them just how good they were – each and every one of them who'd brought England to the brink of the World Cup qualification. I remember some of the pictures had been cut to the music of the M People track 'Search for the Hero inside Yourself'. It made me shiver with excitement.

⚽

Career Highlights

⚽ *England international: 53 caps, 8 goals, England manager 1996–1999*

⚽ *2 FA Cups (1981 and 1982) and a UEFA Cup (1984) with Tottenham • French Championship (1988) with Monaco*

Chris Kamara

Although he picked up a Championship winners' medal with Leeds United in 1992, Chris Kamara is now best known for his energetic gantry reports on Sky Sports' 'Soccer Saturday' and his Sunday morning review show 'Goals on Sunday'.

This little tale will leave many, myself included, wondering how I ever made the transition into broadcasting and television after a long career as a footballer and football manager.

As a player I had personally enjoyed a successful 1988/89 season at Stoke City along with, amongst others, my teammate Peter Beagrie. Towards the end of the season both Peter and I were invited along to Radio Stoke, the local radio station, to chat on air about our hopes and aspirations for the following year in football.

We arrived at the Radio Stoke premises early on Friday evening, pleased to have been selected for this bit of extra publicity and looking forward to a home game the next day. The interviewer went quickly through his idea of how the informal chat would go and roughly what questions he would be asking, etc. With a couple of minutes to go before the start he said, "Oh, do you need some cans?"

Without hesitating I said, 'No, no – we have a game tomorrow!!'

Full marks to me for being a true professional the day before a match and – very rare this – refusing a drink (or so I thought), but I had a lot to learn along the way to my present career!

And for those of you, like me at the time, still wondering what 'cans' are – 'cans' is the broadcasting jargon for 'headphones', which I can regularly be seen wearing on Sky Sports these days!

Career Highlights

❂ *Consecutive promotions from Division 4 to Division 2 (1986 and 1987) with Swindon Town*
- *Championship (1992) with Leeds*

Phil Neal

Bob Paisley's first signing in charge of Liverpool turned out to be a remarkable success story. Plucked from lower league obscurity for just £66,000, Phil Neal became one of the most decorated men in English football history, playing alongside fellow Anfield greats Graeme Souness and Emlyn Hughes.

Off the field, Graeme was as nice a bloke as you could wish to meet with a taste for gold jewellery a la Ron Atkinson, expensive clothes and even a gold American Express card. He was at the centre of a group of players who believed that their success as footballers had earned them the right to the good things in life.

Emlyn Hughes was another in this category, but unlike Graeme he always thought that his money should be kept well out of sight. One occasion I'll never forget came during Liverpool's trip to London for the 1977 Cup final against Manchester United. We got to the team's hotel just around the corner from Harrods on the night before the game and when he unpacked his bag Emlyn discovered to his horror that he'd forgotten to pack a pair of shoes to go with his match day suit. Everyone was in fits because stories of Emlyn's meanness were legendary at the club and the prospect of him having to start his match day preparations with the purchase of a new pair of shoes seemed bound to put him in a great frame of mind for the game.

Next morning though, he allowed himself to be pointed in the direction of Harrods for his shopping trip. Half an hour later he was back, complaining that he couldn't find anything that he liked for less than £40 and that there was no way he was going to waste that sort of money when he'd got a perfectly good pair back at home. No one really took him seriously until the time came to leave for Wembley and Emlyn appeared in the lobby dressed in an immaculate grey suit like the rest of us, but wearing a pair of red training shoes instead of conventional footwear!

Career Highlights

⚽ *England international: 50 caps, 5 goals*

⚽ *7 Championships (1976, 1977, 1979, 1980, 1982, 1983 and 1984), 4 League Cups (1981, 1982, 1983 and 1984), 4 European Cups (1977, 1978, 1981 and 1984) and a UEFA Cup (1976) with Liverpool*

Jack Charlton, OBE

John 'Jack' Charlton was an England World Cup winner who spent his entire career at Leeds United, making 773 appearances for them. In 1986 he was a controversial choice as manager of the Republic of Ireland's national team (the first non-Irishman to be appointed) but he was astonishingly successful, winning qualification to two successive World Cup finals.

For the first time, Ireland were within touching distance of the World Cup. We were in the last eight, the last bloody eight! More than that, we were headed for the biggest stage of all, a quarter-final tie against Italy in the Olympic Stadium in Rome.

Within a few hours, I was made to realize that the win over Romania carried a price tag. Mick Byrne, the team physio, was a devout Catholic, all the players in the squad were Catholics – and when we first qualified for the finals, he came to me and said, 'Hey, boss, if we get to Rome, you've got to get us to meet the Pope.' Sure, Mick, no problem!

Part of our entourage on all big occasions was Monsignor Liam Boyle, a fine man who paid all his own travelling expenses, but was otherwise a member of the official party. Any place I've ever been as a manager, I've encouraged the practice of having a padre around, not to preach but just to have a presence. If any players felt they needed to have a word with him, they could go and do so in private.

Mgr Boyle together with Bishop Tony Farquahar, who had travelled out to support us, were the key figures in getting us into the Vatican for an event which would rate as one of the lasting memories of our stay in Italy. To be honest, I wasn't much in favour of the idea when it was first put to me. No disrespect to the Pontiff, but somehow I was apprehensive about all the fuss in going there the day before a big game.

In my naivety, I had this idea that we would be taken into a big room, the Pope would come in, say a prayer or something and leave. Not at all! We were ushered into a vast auditorium, with as many as six or seven thousand people present from all parts of the world. Fortunately, we were close to the side of the stage, just yards away from the papal throne.

Eventually, the Pope entered the chamber in his white robes, read a lesson for perhaps twenty minutes or so, and sat down. Then the bishops who were sat alongside him translated the lesson into various languages. It must have gone on for two or two and a half hours. I was hot and tired, and as we sat there, my eyes started to close. I was conscious of the battery of press

continued...

Jack Charlton, OBE

continued...

photographers on the other side of the stage targeting us, and the last thing in the world I wanted was for Jack Charlton to nod off during his audience with the Pope! I could imagine the picture appearing on the front page of the Sun or the Mirror – and the caption, which would go with it.

But I tell you, it was hard work staying awake. The Pope, apparently, has to do this three or four times a week, and from my brief experience, it takes some doing. Every so often, he'd cover his face with his hands, scratch behind his ear, or wipe his forehead, and at intervals of ten minutes or so, he'd make a sign of the cross to the audience, first to the left of the chamber, then the centre, and so on. I must have dozed off and he must have been on the third part of his blessing – but when I woke up, he was looking at me with his hand raised. And I swear to God, I thought he was waving at me. So I half stood up and waved back at him! The photographers didn't twig it, and hell, was I happy they didn't. Picture my embarrassment if they had!

Career Highlights

- *England international: 35 caps, 6 goals, Republic of Ireland manager 1986–1995*
- *World Cup (1966) • Championship (1969), FA Cup (1972), League Cup (1968) and 2 UEFA Cups (1968 and 1971) with Leeds*

Joe Corrigan

Joe Corrigan was a giant of a man, with his 6ft 5inch, 15 stone frame. It belied a remarkable agility and amazingly quick reflexes. He could dominate games and turn matches, but will always be remembered as England's third-choice goalkeeper. And for that, you have to blame a certain Ray Clemence and Peter Shilton.

During an England 'B' tour of Malaysia, New Zealand and Singapore the team was invited to a lunch in Singapore sponsored by the Far Eastern division of the Guinness Co. After the lunch and presentation had finished the lads decided to ask to stay on for an hour or so and enjoy a bit more local hospitality. After a while John Hollins and I, the two senior members of the squad, saw the time and took charge of getting the boys back to the hotel to prepare for a dinner party at the Singapore High Commission. Anyone who has been to that great city will know that it is nearly impossible to get a taxi for one, never mind for 18 people, but after a little help from our friends from Guinness we managed to get everyone sorted out and en route to the hotel, with the exception of John and myself. We stood waiting on the side of the road for ages, but as the rush hour hit full swing, our chances of getting back looked less and less likely. By this stage we were in danger of being really late for the reception, so we hit on the idea of getting a bike rickshaw to take us back.

We managed to flag one down and got into the contraption, but because there were two of us, and our combined weight was over 27 stone, the poor man, no matter how much he huffed and puffed, could not get the thing moving. In desperation I decided the only thing to do was ride it myself. I eventually persuaded the driver to get into the rickshaw with John, and we headed at some pace to the hotel. It must have been quite a sight – a 6ft 5in. giant pedalling furiously through the streets of Singapore with an Englishman and a Chinese sitting in the back of his rickshaw. To add to the comedy of the scene, the delighted Chinaman proceeded to light a cigarette and lay back regally in his seat to wave to all his amazed friends.

Career Highlights

⚽ *England international: 9 caps*

⚽ *Championship (1968), 2 League Cups (1970 and 1976), FA Cup (1969) and a European Cup Winners' Cup (1970) with Manchester City*

George Graham

George Graham has had a hugely successful career both as a player and a manager. His greatest triumphs came as manager of Arsenal, but he spent part of the 1960s playing at another famous London club – Chelsea.

Terry Venables was the biggest influence on the Chelsea team. Even at twenty-one he was a natural leader and he patrolled our midfield with a Napoleonic air, feeding the ball through to nippy front-runners with superbly delivered passes. It was a mutual love of good music that first laid the foundation to our friendship.

After training at Mitcham, Terry, John Hollins, Ron Harris and I often used to call in on Chelsea fan Pat Sherlock, who helped run Mills Music in Tin Pan Alley's Denmark Street. As soon as we arrived in his office he would shout out, 'Reg, get the tea.' Reg, a tubby young lad with glasses, would bring four mugs of tea and then start trying to tell us why Watford were a better team than Chelsea. Some years later when I was at Heathrow with the Scotland team an unbelievable vision came towards me wearing silver, high-heeled boots, a purple fur coat and huge, gold-framed spectacles. 'Do you want me to get you a mug of tea, George?' He asked. It was, of course Elton John, who I had known as Reg Dwight in his office boy days. I was with him in a boardroom when he was Watford chairman ten years later, and kept calling him Reg. He pulled me to one side and said 'George, do us a favour. Call me Elton. Reg is not quite the right image!'

Career Highlights

- Scotland international: 12 caps, 3 goals
- League Cup (1965) with Chelsea • League Championship and FA Cup (1971) and a UEFA Cup (1970) with Arsenal • 2 Championships (1989 and 1991), FA Cup (1993), 2 League Cups (1987 and 1993) and a European Cup Winners' Cup (1994) with Arsenal (manager) • League Cup (1999) with Tottenham (manager)

Brendon Batson, MBE

Brendon Batson made almost 350 appearances for Cambridge United and West Bromwich Albion during the 1970s and 1980s. Following his playing career he joined the PFA, rising to the post of Deputy Chief Executive. A man of great integrity, Brendon was awarded the MBE by the Queen in 2001.

In May 1978, West Bromwich Albion were the first British team to embark on a tour to China where we were to play four matches across the country. Travelling with the team were the BBC World About Us television crew who were filming the ground breaking tour.

Whilst there, we were taken to visit the Great Wall, one of the wonders of the world stretching in excess of 4000 miles from the east to the west of China. As we were admiring the spectacular view the presenter of the World About Us programme asked Mick Martin, an Irish international player and one of the great wits of the team, what he thought of the Great Wall.

Quick as a flash Mick replied, 'I've bent balls round bigger walls than this.'

Career Highlights

- *A figurehead for major campaigns against racism and drug abuse in football*
- *As a member of West Brom's trio the 'Three Degrees', Brendon was regarded as an inspirational role model for black players*

Peter Bonetti

Such was the reputation of Peter 'the Cat' Bonetti that Pelé once went on record as saying, 'The three greatest goalkeepers I have ever seen are Gordon Banks, Lev Yashin and Peter Bonetti.' He was understudy to the great Banks at the time of England football's greatest triumph.

During the 1966 World Cup campaign, I, along with the rest of the squad, were staying in a hotel called Hendon Hall in north London. It was where the England team always stayed when we were on international duty. The hotel was ancient and it was one of those places where the staff seemed to be as old as the building. On the top floor, there were two attic rooms that faced each other – I always shared one of the rooms with Ron Springett, and Alan Ball and Nobby Stiles would share the other.

Now, back in those days if you were sponsored by boot companies it was organized on a pay-as-you-play basis, which was simply, if you played a lot, you got paid a lot. More importantly, the money was given to you in cash, and for us back then these cash payments were a pretty big deal. Being second choice goalkeeper behind Gordon Banks, I was usually on the bench, and after one particular game during the tournament, when neither Ron or I had played, Bally and Nobby came up to the top floor full of it: 'look how much money we've got' they taunted, flashing huge wads of cash in our faces. They kept on and on at us, running around shouting 'you haven't got any, look at all this money!' After several minutes of this ribbing, Springett just stood up, snatched the money out of Bally's hand and calmly threw it out of the open window. Bally's face dropped as he gawped at the thick bundles of cash quickly spreading out on the breeze and cascading down towards the street below. Ron and I simply watched in delight. Bally spent the rest of the evening scrambling furiously around the pavements of north London trying to gather it all up. It was very funny, and he was a little more discreet after that!

Career Highlights

⚽ *England international: 7 caps*

⚽ *FA Cup (1970), League Cup (1965) and a European Cup Winners' Cup (1971) with Chelsea*

Tony Adams, MBE

Tony Adams is an England and Arsenal legend – an inspirational captain for both club and country. His successful battle with alcoholism is well documented and universally admired.

On long get-togethers with England, from a Thursday through to the following Wednesday before important internationals, Bobby Robson would take us to a local pub to relax, which naturally I enjoyed. Graham Taylor also took us to a restaurant one night and after checking that it was OK to drink, I did – plenty. I got very lippy by the end of the evening and was giving all the Liverpool lads an earful about 1989. So obnoxious was I being, apparently, that David Seaman and Mark Wright had to pin me down on the back seat, David putting his hand over my mouth to shut me up.

Career Highlights

⚽ *England international: 66 caps, 5 goals*

⚽ *3 Championships (1989, 1991 and 1998), 2 FA Cups (1993 and 1998), 2 League Cups (1987 and 1993) and a European Cup Winners' Cup (1994) with Arsenal*

Sami Hyypia

Dominant in the air, cool under pressure and good on the ball, the towering Finn was soon elevated to the status of Kop legend when he moved to Anfield in 1999. His Liverpool legacy was secured when he helped the club to Champions League glory in 2005.

There was an interesting little incident once during a Finland away fixture against Albania. When the Finland international squad were preparing for their journey home, the personnel at Tirana airport in Albania refused to refuel the airplane unless the fuel was paid for in cash. Moreover, they would only accept US dollars. Needless to say, the pilots and crew didn't have the required amount of cash with them, so the money had to be collected from the players and other passengers on the plane. Somehow, the Finland team managed to collect enough US dollars to pay for the fuel, and the plane departed for Finland soon after.

I have to say that it was a very bizarre experience – an airline collecting money from the passengers to get enough fuel to fly back! I'm sure the money would have been easier to collect if they had asked for British pounds, but fortunately some of us had enough US dollars to get us out of Albania. I'm sure we would have felt a bit forlorn if we had had to stay there, especially because we were going to play Greece in Helsinki in only few days. How strange would that have been – arriving at our home fixture late because the airline didn't have enough money to buy fuel for the return flight.

Career Highlights

⚽ *Finland international: 68 caps, 4 goals*

⚽ *Finnish FA Cup (1992) with MyPa Anjalankoski • Historic 'Quintuplet' – FA Cup, League Cup, Charity Shield, UEFA Cup and European Super Cup (2001) and a European Cup (2005) with Liverpool*

John Aldridge

John Aldridge enjoyed huge success at Oxford United, Liverpool, Spanish side Real Sociedad and Tranmere Rovers. He finally hung up his boots in 1998, shortly before his 40th birthday by which stage he had made 882 career appearances and scored 474 goals.

When I was 14 years old, I went training at the Liverpool football academy every Tuesday and Thursday after school. There was a big group of us lads, and after a month or two of the training, we were all going to be told our fate by Tom Saunders the youth team coach. He sat us all around him, and he pointed at each of us in turn, either saying he'd see us next week, or that we weren't good enough.

Eventually he got to me, and he said 'John, great goal you scored against the B Team. You're definitely coming back, I'll give you a call.'

He was true to his word. Fifteen years later he called – and it cost Liverpool £750,000!

Career Highlights

⚽ *Republic of Ireland international: 69 caps, 19 goals, 4th highest goalscorer of all time*

⚽ *League Cup (1986) with Oxford United • Championship (1988) and FA Cup (1989) with Liverpool*

Match Day

Trevor Francis

England's first million-pound player, Trevor Francis was a stylish striker who was famed for his penalty box skills. He joined Birmingham in June 1969, and quickly established his name by scoring four goals in a League match aged just 16. He was capped more than 50 times for England.

A little story from my England days when the great Sir Bobby Robson was in charge of the national side. As England manager, and throughout his illustrious career, Sir Bobby was always famous for being hopeless with names – he either mixes them up or forgets them altogether.

In the final team meeting before an evening international, in which I was to play up front with Mark Hateley, Sir Bobby was giving us our individual instructions. We leant forward and listened intently, while Sir Bobby earnestly explained that he wanted to get the ball delivered up as early as possible to Tony Hateley and Trevor Whymark. As he carried on enthusiastically in this vein, the rest of the squad and staff were left wondering at what point Mark's father and the former Ipswich player Whymark had been drafted into the starting line up! It was a hell of a muddle to get himself into and goes to show even the most respected and successful managers are only human behind closed doors. Sir Bobby's dawning comprehension made us all laugh, and the ribbings carried on for a long while after that.

Career Highlights

⚽ *England international: 52 caps, 12 goals*

⚽ *League Cup (1980) and a European Cup (1979) with Nottingham Forest • Italian Cup (1985) with Sampdoria • Scottish League Cup (1988) with Rangers*

Dario Gradi, MBE

As the longest serving manager in English football, Dario Gradi was rewarded with an MBE in 1998. His managerial career started at Wimbledon and he went on to pioneer the much-envied Crewe Youth Academy that has launched the career of many Premiership stars.

Some years ago when managing Wimbledon in the old Fourth Division we were playing at Aldershot. Just before the game there was a knock on the dressing room door, 'Who's there?' I asked. 'Tommy McAnearney' came the reply from their manager. Quick as a flash, one of my players called out, 'Come in the three of you!'

NB 'Tommy Mac and Ernie'

Career Highlights

- Britain's longest serving manager (1983–present) with Crewe Alexandra. When he took over his job was to keep them in the Football League, they are now established in the Championship

Niall Quinn, MBE

The Irish gentle giant's Republic of Ireland goalscoring record was only recently eclipsed by Robbie Keane. During his distinguished club and international career, he was as famed for his big heart as he was for his big frame.

Jack Charlton, who I had the pleasure of playing under during my international career, was definitely from the old school of management. I remember one occasion, during preparation for matches against Austria and Latvia, when his lack of understanding of technology or modern methods left the whole team in absolute stitches.

As the team assembled to get Jack's rundown on our opponents we expected even him to pull out a clipboard or at least a pad of paper, but we were stunned when he produced a crumpled old fag packet from his pocket, flattened it out on the table and then squinted at it as if it was written in secret code.

At this point we were all doing anything we could to stop laughing – biting hands, clenching jaws, squeezing chair legs – and some of us were actually struggling to breathe at all!

We could see Jack getting more and more wound up by his inability to read his 'notes', until finally he announced, still squinting desperately: 'Ah bollocks to it. I've written down their strengths and weaknesses from one to eleven, but I haven't said which one's Austria and which one's Latvia! Listen lads,' he said, 'There's nowt for it – I'll do this lot on the left, and if it's Latvia and not Austria, it's not the end of the world, as we're playing them in a couple of weeks anyway aren't we?'

Well, by now we were paralysed by our desperate attempts not to collapse in hysterics – tears rolled down our cheeks, and I for one thought I was going to wet myself. Jack carried on trying to read from his fag packet: 'Goalkeeper, flaps at crosses. Right back, decent player. Left back, struggles for pace. Big centre backs. Six runs … six runs. Um – six runs?' Jack peered at the tiny words and frowned 'Bloody hell, either some buggah has made six decent runs, or the number six likes to run around a lot.'

continued…

Niall Quinn, MBE

continued...

That was it, we could not hold it in for one more second. In unison we fell off our chairs, crying, wailing, holding our sides and desperately trying to catch our breath. Poor old Jack: 'Bollocks to you. All I'm trying to do is help you! Bugger off, the lot of you.'

The truth is, of course, that it was this sense of fun and team unity that Jack had instilled in the Irish set-up, and that served us so well down the years.

Career Highlights

⊕ *Republic of Ireland international: 91 caps, 21 goals, 2nd highest goalscorer of all time*

⊕ *Championship (1989) and League Cup (1987) with Arsenal*

Chris Coleman

Having only hung up his boots as a player in 2002, Chris Coleman became the youngest manager in the history of the Premiership and proceeded to guide Fulham to their highest ever League finish in his first season. As a centre back, he was inspirational in Fulham's meteoric rise through the Football League to the Premiership, as well as featuring regularly for the Welsh national side.

L ike most professional footballers I've been on the receiving end of an inspirational team talk or two in my career, but one in particular sticks in my mind for all the wrong reasons. Bobby Gould, then manager of Wales, had called the national team together for a crisis meeting; things were going from bad to worse for us and a run of defeats had really shattered morale.

We walked in to find Bobby quite fired up, and, like a general addressing an invading army, he proceeded to lay out before us his dramatic vision for a new era in Welsh football. 'Things are about to change,' he began, 'the whole experience of being part of this set-up must be revolutionized.'

He had our attention: 'we need to be more professional in every minute aspect of our organization. To this end we are going to train like we have never trained before and we are going to employ specialist coaches to address all areas of our game. We are going to stay in the very top hotels before games, we will adopt the best, most up-to-date nutritional programmes and we will use the newest, smartest playing kit and equipment. We are an elite, professional unit,' he said forcefully, 'and it's high time we started to look, feel and act like one.'

The lads were on the edge of their seats. This was exactly what we all needed: passion, pride and a sense that the Welsh FA were willing to create an elite, professional environment for its players to flourish in.

'We,' boomed Bobby with a final, rousing flourish, 'are going to start thinking like Brazil, acting like Brazil, playing like Brazil and winning like Brazil. And we can achieve this by attending to every tiny detail of our organization with rigorous, determined professionalism.'

As Bobby's impassioned speech came to an end we cheered our unreserved approval. Upbeat, energized and with renewed steel in our eyes and our hearts we climbed aboard the team bus.

It wouldn't start.

Career Highlights

⚽ *Wales international: 32 caps, 4 goals*

⚽ *Youngest Premiership manager aged 32 (Fulham)*

Terry Butcher

As a competitive and commanding centre-half, Terry Butcher had an illustrious international and domestic career. He enjoyed success under Sir Bobby Robson at Ipswich and played a major part in the resurgence of Rangers during the late 1980s.

You soon get to know your opponents whether from international games, social functions or just playing against each other regularly. I always like to talk to the man I'm marking and ask how they are doing, how their family is and so on or share a moan about the pitch, the weather or the referee. A little chat can also serve another purpose in helping you gauge how you stand with your opponent psychologically. From what they say you can usually tell whether they are in the mood to play or not.

I have heard some centre-halves take it even further and say things to their opponent like: 'How much money are you earning?' Whatever the reply, the centre-half will then say: 'is that all! Well so and so told me he's on double that and his team are down the bottom of the table.' If they are convincing enough they get their opponent more concerned about his wages than he is with what's happening in the game.

As Captain you always have a chat with the opposing skipper when you go up for the toss. Some players appear quite relaxed while others are obviously tense and it's normally nothing more than a quick 'hello' and 'all the best'. Before one game against Liverpool, I was shaking hands with Phil Neal who was their captain at the time. I had just opened my insurance business in Ipswich and asked Phil if he had any insurance. I could see that he looked puzzled. Then I whipped out a calling card from the company and said: 'Give me a call if you need any – the phone number's on the card,' and ran back for the kick-off, leaving a bemused Phil standing on the centre-spot not knowing what to do with the card.

Career Highlights

⚽ *England international: 77 caps, 3 goals*

⚽ *UEFA Cup (1981) with Ipswich • 3 Scottish Championships (1987, 1989 and 1990) and 2 Scottish League Cups (1987 and 1989) with Rangers*

Mick McCarthy

Mick McCarthy has been an inherent part of Irish football since the early 1980s. He was capped over 50 times for his country and rose to the challenge when he was handed the apparently impossible task of replacing the great Jack Charlton as manager in 1996.

I was called up to the Republic of Ireland squad for the first time in 1984. We had a match at Lansdowne Road against Poland and were then due to depart for Japan where we were competing in the Kirin Challenge Cup.

Before our departure, our manager, Eoin Hand, told us that throughout our trip we were all ambassadors of Ireland and were to make good impressions on the locals. He said that our international reputation, both on and off the field, was of great importance and we were to do everything we could to maintain a high standard of courtesy. We carried out his instructions by signing autographs, posing for photographs and approaching the whole occasion in good spirits. For me, it was my debut on foreign soil so as well as making good impressions off the field, I wanted to make a good impression on it.

Our first fixture was against the Japan Universiade XI, and before the warm up, the manager again gave us a pep talk on our conduct and behaviour. He told us to play like gentlemen and acknowledge the crowd as we emerged from the tunnel to try and get them behind us.

As I prepared to go out for a warm up, I could hear the crowd cheering around the stadium. It wasn't a big crowd, maybe only six or seven thousand, but there were television cameras and I was determined to make them remember Mick McCarthy. There were a few steps leading up to the pitch and having negotiated them, I made my way out onto the athletics track that ran around the perimeter of the pitch. I turned as I jogged over the track and was just making to wave my hand at the supporters behind me when I tripped on the inside rim. To say I fell over or stumbled would be an understatement. The truth is, I fell arse over tit. And as I lay in a crumpled heap on the edge of the pitch all I could hear was thousands of Japanese fans laughing their heads off and trying to take pictures of me between their uncontrollable giggles.

continued...

Mick McCarthy

continued...

I was dying of embarrassment as I gathered myself up and trotted self-consciously out to join my teammates. But to this day, at least I know that I carried out my managers' orders. He told us to make lasting impressions, and I certainly did that. Maybe not how I'd anticipated, but I made an impression all the same and enjoyed a healthy cheer whenever I touched the ball during the game.

Career Highlights

❂ *Republic of Ireland international: 57 caps, 2 goals, Republic of Ireland manager 1996-2002*

❂ *Scottish Championship (1988) and 2 Scottish Cups (1988 and 1989) with Celtic • Promotion to the Premiership (2005) with Sunderland (manager)*

Cyrille Regis

Cyrille Regis was part of the generation of black players in the 1970s and 1980s who paved the way for the likes of Ian Wright, John Barnes and Paul Ince. The powerful centre-forward was a Midlands legend with West Brom, Coventry, Aston Villa and Wolves and won five England caps between 1982 and 1988.

In 1978/79, during my first season in the professional game, I was playing for West Bromwich Albion. Late on in the campaign, we were playing in a cup game away at West Ham. The score was 2–0 in their favour and during the second half, Ron Atkinson, the then manager, was forced to make some changes so he brought on Tony 'Bomber' Brown. He came running up to me with a curious expression on his face and asked, 'Which way are we kicking?' I pointed my finger and replied, 'that way.' I called him a few choice words as he jogged away laughing his head off!

Career Highlights

- England international: 5 caps
- FA Cup (1987) with Coventry

John Fashanu

John Fashanu was a bustling centre-forward who made his name in the Wimbledon 'Crazy Gang' during the late 1980s. He retired in 1995 after two England caps and an FA Cup winner's medal. Since then, his gregarious personality has made him a natural in front of the television cameras.

Vinny Jones not only had one of the longest throws in the game of football but also one of the greatest sense of humours. During our Wimbledon days together, I remember one afternoon where he combined both these traits in a game against Manchester United. We had a throw-in just inside the United half and Vinny used to do this wonderful thing where he'd walk back into the stands in order to get a good powerful run up. On this occasion however, he walked into the stand and unbeknownst to us, walked around the back of it, into the tunnel and down into the dressing room. The layout of the stadium meant that everyone was oblivious to what he had done. Five minutes of puzzlement ensued – a long time in the context of a Premiership game – and when it began to dawn on us that Vinny wasn't coming back from the stand, the referee instigated a manhunt. Having eventually traced him to the home dressing room, where Vinny sat clutching the ball and giggling to himself, the referee booked him for his troubles. It was absolutely hilarious and a typical Jonesy stunt.

Career Highlights

✪ *England international: 2 caps*

✪ *FA Cup (1988) with Wimbledon*

John Motson, OBE

'Motty' is the voice of British football. He was awarded his OBE for his services to sports broadcasting and remains one of the nation's favourite commentators.

One of the more extraordinary things that I have witnessed during my commentating career took place in April 1977. It was a game between Derby County and Manchester City at Derby's old stadium, The Baseball Ground. The pitch was notorious for being extremely muddy, and with Derby County leading the match 2-0, the referee awarded a penalty to the home side. It became apparent, however, that the box was such a quagmire that the penalty spot had been completely obscured. Joe Corrigan informed the referee of this problem, and was promptly booked for his insolence. The referee then noticed that he too could not find the spot and for a moment everyone paused and just looked around at each other in puzzlement.

Luckily, the head groundsman Bob Smith was close at hand and it was eventually decided that he be called upon to paint a new spot. Dressed utterly inappropriately in a flared corduroy suit - much to the amusement of the watching crowd - he ran-walked around the perimeter of the ground, with a bucket of white paint sloshing by his side. The referee, meanwhile, busily tried to pace out the twelve yards. All eyes in the stadium where fixed on poor Bob Smith, as the players were ushered to one side and he carefully painted the offending spot back. Gerry Daly stepped up and scored for Derby. The final outcome was 4-0 to the home side but the bizarre penalty spot has always been what the game was remembered for.

Career Highlights

⊛ *Between 1979 and 1994, Motson was the BBC's TV commentator for 29 consecutive major cup finals including FA Cups, World Cups and European Championships*

⊛ *John Motson has covered well over 1,000 football matches for the BBC*

Sir Trevor Brooking, KBE

A gentleman in a rough game and an authentic English sporting hero, the great Sir Trevor Brooking spent his entire career playing for his beloved West Ham United.

No club in the Football League has such an affinity with its fans as West Ham. It is truly a family club, and the 24,000 fans who regularly attend matches at Upton Park are part of that family. At each home game the mascot leads the team out and is usually given an encouraging reception. There is one that stands out in my memory, a fair haired boy of six who was mascot for the FA Cup tie against Wrexham on 3rd January 1981. The 30,000 crowd (an amazing attendance in view of the opposition) really took to him and roared encouragement as he dribbled up to Phil Parkes and 'scored' from close range. During the match Frank Lampard Sr. was injured and needed treatment. While Rob Jenkins, the physiotherapist, was swabbing down his nose, the whole stadium broke into song and chanted: 'bring on the mascot!'

Career Highlights

✪ *England international: 47 caps, 5 goals*

✪ *FA Cup (1980) with West Ham*

Kevin Phillips

Kevin Phillips established a reputation as one of the most dangerous forwards in England by scoring 115 times in 209 league games during his six-year spell with Sunderland.

I was playing for Sunderland in the 1997/98 season. We eventually reached the play-offs, but before that, while still gunning for an automatic promotion place, we met Bradford at Valley Parade in a crucial top-two battle.

The rain was lashing down as we drove into the city, and we all feared the effect it would be having on the heavy Valley Parade surface, not the greatest at the best of times. The game went ahead however, and was a tight, hard-fought affair. It also went on to produce what I think would be a cracking Question of Sport question: 'Who is the only Sunderland player to score a goal and keep a clean sheet in the same game?'

The answer? Niall Quinn. I was having quite a good game, but it was Quinny who headed us into the lead with half an hour remaining. We were looking good, until Thomas Sorensen got a knock and had to be carried off. With no reserve keeper on the bench, victory, and potentially the title, were hanging in the balance.

Who was going to step between the posts? Being 5ft 7 I was glad to be out of the running, but the debate was settled when Quinny, calm as ever, strode over to the bench and pulled on the gloves. He had a blinder, actually pulling off a couple of crucial saves. He came off the pitch to a hero's reception!

Career Highlights

- ✪ *England international, 8 caps*

- ✪ *Promotion to the Premiership (1999) • European Golden Boot (2000) as the Continent's top striker with Sunderland*

Paul McGrath

A tough but talented centre-half, the former Manchester United and Aston Villa player is one of the most capped Irishmen of all time. No player in Ireland's history has had so many column inches written in his honour, yet Paul always remained modest about his ability.

These days footballers are looked upon as almost superhuman, but here's an embarrassing story that shows how very human we are! One particular season at Manchester United we had been enjoying our best start for many years, winning all of our first ten games. The next game was away at Ipswich Town, and the club flew us down in two tiny planes. I hate flying anyway, and these little contraptions scared the hell out of me – I walked off the plane with my stomach in absolute knots. Despite all the careful match preparations I was still feeling extremely dodgy down there when kick-off arrived, and just felt worse and worse as the time went on.

As the match entered its closing stages, things were getting pretty desperate and I was virtually crossing my legs to keep everything in place. It didn't help that the opposition kept launching balls over the top which I had to jump to defend. I complained frantically to my defensive teammates about the seriousness of the situation, but they kept telling me to stop being soft and get on with it – there was only eight or nine minutes to go after all. At that point it suddenly dawned on me that if I didn't leave that pitch immediately, I was going to lose control of my stomach there and then, and would never be able to show my face in public, let alone on a football pitch, ever again. So, to the utter astonishment of players, coaches and fans alike I turned away from the action, trotted silently up the touch line – past a very miffed looking Ron Atkinson – and down the tunnel. I never made it back onto the pitch and, because I was never substituted, we finished the game with ten men. Thank God we won 1–0. My teammates, of course, had an absolute field day afterwards, but as I sat in the bath taking their jibes, I felt nothing but sweet relief.

Career Highlights

❖ *Republic of Ireland international: 83 caps, 8 goals*

❖ *FA Cup (1985) with Manchester United*

Brian McClair

Brian 'Choccy' McClair was a devoted servant of Manchester United for 11 years. The Scotsman was a potent force in English football and, alongside Mark Hughes, paved the way for much of United's early success in the 1990s.

The away dressing room at Upton Park is at the front of the ground, and people can walk along by it. Fans can actually see down into it. During the sacred moments that are the team talk, it was very warm in there and we opened the window to let in a bit of air. West Ham fans were looking in and shouting out while the Gaffer was holding forth. Someone boomed out, 'What's the difference between a Scotsman and a coconut? You can get a drink out of a coconut.' The manager had been concentrating so hard on what he was saying, he didn't hear what had been said to make his players fall about laughing. Brian Kidd repeated it and the Gaffer joined in the laughter.

Career Highlights

- *Scotland international: 27 caps, 2 goals*
- *Scottish Cup (1985) and League Championship (1986) with Celtic*
- *4 Championships (1993, 1994, 1996 and 1997), 2 FA Cups (1990 and 1994), League Cup (1992) and a European Cup Winners' Cup (1991) with Manchester United*

Steve Bull, MBE

Remarkably, Steve Bull was capped by England while playing in the old Third Division. Steve is a bona fide legend at Wolverhampton Wanderers; he scored 306 goals for the club, 100 of them coming in just two seasons.

It is amazing in football how often a seemingly silly lighthearted moment can help to pull a bunch of players together when the chips are down. One of the funniest such incidents that I can remember was during a Wolves game. After a dismal first half we were 3–0 down and all walked into the dressing room with our heads hanging hopelessly low.

Graham Taylor was manager at the time and was giving us an absolute roasting. As he tore into us though, one by one our attention turned to the bloke sitting behind him – our right back at the time, 'Digger' Barnes. Digger had stuck a piece of black plastic between his front teeth and was grinning like an idiot behind Graham's back. Eventually, with the furious team talk still in full flow, everyone's eyes were fixed on Digger's performance, and you know what it's like when you're not meant to laugh – we were all sniggering uncontrollably and on the verge of collapse. Graham finally twigged and went mad, throwing around pots and pans and screaming at Digger. I know you shouldn't really laugh at times like that, and the manager didn't see the funny side of it at all, but I don't recall him complaining when we went out for the second half and won the game 4–3.

Career Highlights

⚽ *England international: 13 caps, 4 goals*

⚽ *545 full appearances, scoring 306 goals for Wolves including a record 18 hat-tricks*

Howard Wilkinson

Howard Wilkinson has been deeply involved in the national game for many years. He is the former Technical Director of the FA, current Chairman of the League Managers' Association and is the only person to have managed the England national team on two separate occasions. At Notts County, he was given his start as a Football League manager.

During the 1980/81 season, I was made team manager of Notts County under the legendary Scot, Jimmy Sirrel. Jimmy was one of the game's great characters, an inimitable personality who, like Bill Shankly and Brian Clough, was moulded in his own particular way. He had been involved at Meadow Lane for many years and in his capacity of club manager, he appointed me head coach of the first team. The arrangement between us was simple and suited us both; I was in charge of all team affairs and he wouldn't interfere in any way, unless I specifically asked.

To the astonishment of the football experts at the time, Notts County had a great start to the season and we soon found ourselves joint top after an impressive string of results. More importantly, we were still there at the end of the season finishing in second place behind West Ham and winning promotion to the old First Division.

Our unbeaten start was under threat however; our next fixture was a tough game away to the eventual champions. The timing was good though, with the team spirit high, we all felt we could get a result. It was a typically hot autumn Saturday and as the players took to the field, it was with real enthusiasm that I took my place in the dugout while Jimmy, as usual, sat a few rows back in the stands behind me.

My optimism was short-lived, as after just 15 minutes, we were struggling. We were being beaten in all areas of the park and were 3–0 down in no time. In fact, such was the Hammers' superiority, it could have been eight and I was desperate for half-time to come so I could reassess the situation. I felt that if I could get the boys in the dressing room, I could make some changes, say a few stern words and send them back out with a hope of salvaging a result.

No such luck. As the second half resumed, nothing I had said or done had worked – the situation was the same, possibly even worse, with West Ham putting our goal under constant attack. I was a young manager, and as I stood on the touchline searching in vain for a solution, I began to think that if ever there was a time I needed a little advice, it was then. While I was pondering over whether to ditch my pride and seek out Jimmy, I suddenly

continued...

Howard Wilkinson

continued…

noticed him out of the corner of my eye standing in the entrance to the tunnel. He wasn't moving; he was just standing there, leaning casually against the wall. He'd left his seat in the stands, and was clearly debating whether to come over and 'interfere'. I didn't want to appear to be losing control but inwardly I was willing him to come and sit down and at least give me a clue. He did. Eventually, he wandered out of the tunnel, past the physio and coaching staff and took a seat on the bench next to me. However, he didn't say anything for a minute or two, he just sat there quietly. We were both chewing our bottom lips, him not wanting to step in, and I not wanting to admit I needed counsel. Finally, he opened his mouth: 'Howard, I know I said I wou'nae interfere wi' the football business, but perhaps I could offer a bit of advice?'

I didn't answer immediately, I left it a cool ten seconds to avoid seeming desperate before answering.

'OK, what do you think?' I asked.

There was another pause.

'Howard, if I were you, I would tell the driver to start the f★★★★★g bus.'

Career Highlights

✪ *England manager, February 1999 and again, October 2000*

✪ *Promotion from Division 2 (1990) and Championship (1992) with Leeds*

Stuart Pearce, MBE

After an illustrious playing career, where he established himself as an uncompromising defender with a cannon shot, Stuart Pearce eventually hung up his boots at Manchester City in 2002. 'Psycho' stayed at the club as a coach and was appointed manager in 2005. He has every chance of being a successful coach after working under the guidance of Brian Clough for many years.

One time, when we had just beaten Queen's Park Rangers in the quarter-final of the League Cup, a group of supporters ran on to the pitch celebrating. Clough hated supporters on his pitch and he lashed out at them, landing punches on two or three of them. Those lads made a big fuss, threatened to sue him and have him arrested. In typical fashion he invited them into the club on Monday morning where they met the players. If they thought that they had been called in for an apology they had another think coming. Clough laid into them, telling them that they shouldn't have been on the pitch. He didn't apologise, but they did.

Who else would have got away with that? Instead of being pilloried, he received letters of support from a Chief of Police and Labour leader Neil Kinnock, and the FA offered to hold the resultant tribunal in Nottingham instead of London! He was fined and briefly banned from the touchline.

Career Highlights

- *England international: 78 caps, 5 goals*
- *2 League Cups (1989 and 1990) with Nottingham Forest*

Neil Warnock

The irrepressible Neil Warnock has done it all in the Football League, presiding over promotion and relegation battles alike. In the early 1990s he took Notts County from the Third Division to the First.

I remember an incident when I was manager of Notts County and we played Ron Atkinson's Aston Villa side. Everyone knows Big Ron likes to look his best, and on this day he was his usual suited and booted self, complete with wide sunglasses and huge, expensive looking overcoat.

During the course of the game, I was annoyed by a poor linesman's decision and begun yelling at him, as you do! As I was disagreeing with the linesman, I could see Ron walking towards me shouting and pointing his match programme. The two dugouts used to be separated by a fairly high wall, and so you could only see the top half of the people on the other side. Ron, or at least Ron's well-groomed top half, was striding towards our dugout with real intent, and I could see he was planning on coming round the wall to have a proper go. But suddenly and for no apparent reason he stopped dead in his tracks and went completely silent. He paused for a moment, before turning on his heels, and walking away again. At the end of the game nothing was said and that was that.

A week later I bumped into him and, as is so often the case, things had blown over and we were having a chat when he suddenly said:

'You know what, I was on my way over to you to give you a real earful, but as I was walking along I stepped calf-deep into a big bucket of soapy water – I looked a complete prat. I remember turning to the physio and saying "If you ever tell anyone about this, you'll never get another job!" '

Career Highlights

⚽ *5 Promotions in 10 years • Scarborough (1986) • Notts County (1990 and 1991) • Huddersfield (1995) • Plymouth (1996)*

Les Ferdinand, MBE

Les Ferdinand is one of the English Premiership's all-time great marksmen. During his early career, he spent a season in the Turkish league where he played for Istanbul-based giants Besiktas. He was a huge hit, scoring 21 goals in just 34 games and helping his side to win the Turkish Cup.

When Gordon Milne was manager of Turkish club Besiktas he signed me from QPR. It is a traditional Muslim ritual in Turkey that they sacrifice a lamb for the team, which is meant to bring good luck. But to those players they see as being special, they also give a pigeon to take out into the stadium. They announced my name and gave me the pigeon, and as I went to run out, they dragged me back to dab the lamb's blood on my boots and forehead. Clearly, I had never experienced anything quite like this before. I had half a thought about rubbing it off, but I realised that would be an insult to the fans. They were going mad with excitement as it was. We didn't actually see the lamb being sacrificed in front of us – it was already dead and its throat had been cut – but it was just lying there on the floor of the tunnel. People could see I was a bit uncomfortable with it, but I realised it was their ritual and I had to respect it. I can safely say, though, that it was very different to what I had been used to at Loftus Road.

However, worse was to follow. When a new player gets to the centre of the pitch, he is meant to throw the pigeon in the air as a sign of good luck. So out I ran and I threw the pigeon up in the air and there was a big roar from the crowd. Everything was going all right, or so I thought. But because the pigeon had been cooped up somewhere for so long, its wings were closed and it couldn't fly away. It just dropped out of the air and landed with a thud at my feet.

I picked up the bird straight away – thinking, 'Oh no, what have I done now?' – and launched it into the air. There was silence and down it plunged again onto the floor. Now I thought I'd really done something serious and the fans were going to run on the pitch and lynch me any moment. But this young boy came over and manipulated the bird's wings open, then gave it back to me. This time, I shut my eyes and threw it as high as I could. I heard this big roar and the pigeon began to struggle a bit but finally flew away. I just thought to myself, 'What a relief!'

Career Highlights

- *England international: 17 caps, 5 goals*
- *Turkish FA Cup (1989) with Besiktas • PFA Player of the Year (1996) at Newcastle • League Cup (1999) with Tottenham*

Arsène Wenger, OBE

Little was known in England about the man who had managed Nancy before taking AS Monaco to the French League Championship. A decade down the line and Arsène Wenger has firmly cemented his place in the Arsenal history books.

After the first day as manager of Arsenal back in September 1996, the press quoted the statement – 'I went back to my hotel room and intended to watch Tottenham on television… but fell asleep.' Unaware at the time of why this was such a popular comment, it could be said that this was the beginning of a great rapport with the club and its fans!

Career Highlights

✤ *French Championship (1979) with Strasbourg* • *French Championship (1988) and French Cup (1991) with Monaco (manager)* • *Emperors' Cup (1995) and Super Cup (1996) with Grampus Eight (manager)*

• *3 Championships (1998, 2002 and 2004) and 3 FA Cups (1998, 2002 and 2003) with Arsenal (manager)*

John Gregory

John Gregory had been the surprise choice as the man to succeed Brian Little at Aston Villa midway through the 1997/98 season. However he soon proved his worth, guiding Villa from the lows of the relegation zone to a UEFA Cup place. Known for speaking his mind, Gregory was always 100 per cent committed to the club and was unfortunate not to taste success in the FA Cup Final of 2000 when he was up against Chelsea's foreign legion.

The Walk.

I suppose it is the moment. The single most stirring image from every Cup Final there has ever been. As a supporter, you will know how you have felt if you have been fortunate enough to see your team come out of that tunnel and walk into the Cup final arena.

Well, take that feeling, multiply by 120, add a few thousand and you will get an idea of how it is for us. On the inside looking out, so to speak.

I'll try, but I doubt I will be able to find the words to do it justice. I know, though, that whenever I want, I will be able to close my eyes and remember every second, every sound, even the smell of it.

My heart and mind were locked in their own private war. My mind was saying, 'Get a grip of yourself for Christ's sake – there's a game to be won.' But for the minute or so that it took to walk from the tunnel to that red carpet stretched out before the Royal Box, my mind was fighting a losing battle. My heart was winning hands down.

And those fans. God, those fans.

Such a sea of colour, of claret and blue. I remember, half way out, I was overwhelmed by the desire to break ranks, rush to the perimeters and hug every last one of them. Beautiful. It's the only word I can think of.

We're lined up, Chelsea opposite. And I remember thinking what a fantastic country England must be. It has to be for all that lot over there to come here.

The drum roll before the national anthem and I attract the Chelsea captain's attention.

'Sing up Wisey – you're the only bugger who knows the words,' I shout across to him.

Career Highlights

⚽ *England international: 6 caps*

⚽ *Runner-up in 2000 FA Cup with Aston Villa (manager)*

Sam Allardyce

In his day, Sam Allardyce was a tough and combative centre-half, but he has gone on to make his mark as a canny and resourceful manager. He took over at Bolton Wanderers in October 1999.

Bolton Wanderers reached the First Division play-offs in the 2000/01 season and after beating West Bromwich Albion and Preston North End they returned to the Premiership. Here's a story about the first-leg semi-final tie at West Brom that portrays me as I wish to be seen.

We were 2–0 down, there's only 35 minutes to go and we were in trouble. I turned to Brownie (Phil Brown, Bolton's assistant manager) and said, 'take Colin Hendry off,' and he's replied, 'What? Hendry?' All season, Colin had been a rock for us but that day he couldn't cope, he'd been booked and was one tackle away from being sent off.

Everyone was saying, 'Colin? Are you sure?' I replied, 'Yeah, get him off.' We put Mick Whitlow on and Colin couldn't believe it. But all I was thinking was, another season in the wilderness, more players sold, less money to pay players and staff, we have to turn things around. We were playing with two up front in a 4-4-2, they were playing 5-3-2 and their system was battering ours.

So, again I said to Brownie, 'Take Dean Holdsworth off.' Again he said, 'What? He's our leading goalscorer.'

'Yeah, but we're getting tanked in midfield. I've got to get a midfield three in there to give us a chance. We can't afford to concede another goal and we have to get one back!'

'You're not going to get a goal by taking off your leading scorer,' said Brownie astonished. 'But he ain't getting in the game because we're being outplayed in midfield,' came my response.

So off came Holdsworth, we put three in midfield and played our three fastest players, Bo Hansen, Michael Ricketts and Ricardo Gardner, on their three centre-halves who were big but not the quickest. Our fans booed when we took Holdsworth off.

They weren't booing the team, they were booing me – 'he's lost it this guy, he can't cope. Boo!' However, the game changes course and we score twice in the last nine minutes and it ends 2-2 and then it's cheers all round.

I tell this story for no particular reason other than to say that Sam Allardyce, the old centre-back who paid his dues with hard tackles and firm headers, is a little smarter than you may think!

Career Highlights

⚽ *Division 2 Champions (1978) with Bolton*

⚽ *Promotion to Division 2 (1998) with Notts County (manager) • Promotion to the Premiership (2001) with Bolton (manager)*

Gary Lineker, OBE

Gary Lineker is one of football's gentlemen, not receiving a single yellow card in his entire professional career. A quiet man off the field, on it he was deadly. Gary played 80 times for his country and scored an astonishing 48 goals.

Some years ago, one of my teammates retaliated after being spat on by a player from the opposing team. Our manager's rejoinder to him was, 'In future, if someone spits on you, you just have to swallow it.'

I am not sure that any of us took him seriously!

Career Highlights

- *England international: 80 caps, 48 goals, England's 2nd highest goalscorer of all time*
- *2 Spanish FA Cups (1987 and 1988) and a European Cup Winners' Cup (1989) with Barcelona*
  - *FA Cup (1991) with Tottenham*

Sir Bobby Robson, KBE

English football's elder statesman, Sir Bobby was rewarded for his contribution to the game with a knighthood in 2002. As well as nearly guiding England to a second World Cup in 1990, he has managed some of Europe's most famous clubs.

John Cobbold was the chairman of Ipswich Town between 1957 and 1976. He hired me as manager in 1969 and from that moment always made sure that when we won a game we had a bottle of champagne. However, when we lost a game we always had two!

Career Highlights

- *England international: 20 caps, 4 goals, England manager (1982–1990)*

- *FA Cup (1978) and UEFA Cup (1981) with Ipswich (manager) • 2 Dutch Championships (1991 and 1992) with PSV Eindhoven (manager) • 2 Portuguese Championships (1995 and 1996) and Portuguese Cup (1994) with Porto (manager) • Spanish Cup and a European Cup Winners' Cup (1997) with Barcelona (manager)*

Shaun Bartlett

A celebrity in his native South Africa, Shaun Bartlett received a telephone call from Nelson Mandela asking why he had not been invited to the footballer's wedding ... it's unclear whether the country's postal service was at fault, but anyway the great man was there to watch the striker tie the knot.

Growing up in South Africa under apartheid was never easy nor were the conditions you lived in. Every day there was always a certain amount of violence, whether it was related to the struggle for freedom or just crime. And that's how violence became part of our everyday life.

Now imagine playing a football match under these conditions.

It was in 1997 when we had to go to the Congo for a World Cup qualifying game. We arrived two days before the match as we wanted to spend as little time as possible in the country. The hotel was, as expected, not to the best of standards nor was the food. We had to get by with eating just bread and sometimes sweets for every meal – not exactly the proper preparation for such an important match. Training at the Congolese national team ground was not an option as we were not allowed to get close to that facility. So the small 10m x 20m piece of ground next to the hotel was our training pitch. As you can see, everything was made as difficult for us as possible in order that we failed in our quest to win the game.

Match day arrived and the pitch was surrounded by the army and their loaded AK47 weapons. The first thing we were made aware of was not even to think about winning this game as our lives would not be spared. Needless to say this put us in a more than difficult position. Did we try to win the game and risk our lives (was the threat genuine?) or did we concede defeat and get out of the country as quickly as possible with our lives intact?

Well, we had no choice but to lose the game and make sure that the outcome was in their favour. We lost 2–0, but still managed to qualify for the World Cup in 1998, ironically beating the Congolese in our home country to qualify. What a result. Revenge was sweet!

Whoever said that football is not about going to war, should have been at that game and maybe they would have changed their views!

Lots of love and peace.

Career Highlights

- South African international: 66 caps, 27 goals, South Africa's leading goalscorer of all time
- Swiss Cup (2000) with FC Zurich

After the Final Whistle

Steve Bruce

Steve Bruce was the linchpin of the Manchester United defence for nine years and was the first Englishman to captain a team to a League and Cup double. Now manager of Birmingham City, he has, with some astute signings and good tactical awareness, developed the Midlands club into a solid Premiership outfit.

I won my first Premiership title reclined on a sofa at home with my wife Janet sleeping in the armchair next to me. More astonishingly, when the glorious moment arrived, I, along with every other member of the Manchester United squad, were disobeying direct orders from our manager.

At 5.45 pm on Sunday, 2nd May 1993, Manchester United became the champions of English football for the first time since 1967. It had been a wait of 26 years during which frustrations had built up, hopes had been dashed and patience stretched.

I can remember the marvellous day clearly. We were due to play Blackburn on the Monday; the match was to be shown live on television and everybody thought it would decide the Championship. We were four points clear of our nearest rivals, Aston Villa, and they had a match on the Sunday, at home to lowly Oldham Athletic who needed to win all their remaining fixtures to stay up in their first season in the top flight. With Aston Villa going for the title, Oldham's chances appeared slim at Villa Park, to say the least. Three points for Villa would bring them within one of us, so we needed to win the Blackburn match to secure the title.

These mathematical considerations, as well as our superior goal difference, made us clear favourites. But then, we had been clear favourites twelve months earlier and had still managed to allow Leeds to come through and take the title that we thought was destined to be ours. With this in mind, we were all a bit tense and on edge.

So, on that fateful Sunday morning, we had gone in for a little gentle training to tone us up for the Blackburn match. We had a light lunch then went our separate ways, with the instructions from our manager Alex Ferguson still clear in our minds. He said that none of us were to watch the Villa game on television. He wanted us to concentrate solely on the Blackburn game and did not want us sidetracked by events at Villa Park. Always one to practise what he preached, he disappeared off for a round of golf, while I settled down at home in front of the box to watch it all. So too, all around Manchester did the rest of the players. My wife clearly didn't detect my tension or excitement because when she sat down to watch the game, she promptly fell asleep. She was certainly awake however, when Oldham scored midway through the first half. Nick Henry chose to score his 16th goal in an Oldham shirt against Aston Villa to become the toast of Manchester United fans across the country.

continued...

Steve Bruce

continued...

Yet the Oldham breakthrough was only the beginning of the tension, as the game wore on, the sweat was pouring off me as our chances of winning the title got closer by the second. When the final whistle blew, I suspected I might have a few visitors before long. Peter Schmeichel who lived almost next door rang on the doorbell, quickly followed by Paul Ince and Paul Parker who were also close at hand. Before long the whole team was congregated at the Bruce household for some serious celebrations. I phoned the manager to see if he wanted to come and join in, but he too had guests and declined. I think he heard the carousing going on in the background and chose not to extend an invitation to me and my guests! He did however remind me that we had a game the next day.

As you can imagine it turned into a tremendous party; countless bottles of champagne and wine, several hundred beers and an unspecified number of bottles of spirits were drunk. The party lasted until the next morning and I can tell you there were a few sore heads about.

So, having won the title without kicking a ball and gone against the manager's instructions, I think the most amazing thing of all, was we still managed to beat Blackburn 3-1!

Career Highlights

⚽ *League Cup (1985) with Norwich* • *3 Championships (1993, 1994 and 1996), 3 FA Cups (1990, 1994 and 1996), League Cup (1992) and a European Cup Winners' Cup (1991) with Manchester United*

George Best

Genius, magician, legend, George Best is one of the most naturally gifted players ever to grace a football pitch. Sometimes nicknamed 'the fifth Beatle', he was one of the most famous stars of Britain in the 1960s.

The famous 'George, where did it all go wrong?' story sums it up. I'd been to a casino with Mary Stavin, who had won the Miss World contest shortly before. We'd done well in the casino and I had exchanged my chips for plenty of cash. I think it was close on £20,000. Tucking it into my jacket, we walked back to the Holiday Inn in Birmingham where we were staying. In our room I spread the notes across the bed and began counting the cash as Mary slipped into a negligee. Excited by my good fortune I called down to the night porter for a nice bottle of Dom Pérignon champagne. It was clear from his accent that he too originally hailed from Belfast. When he arrived in the room he placed the champers and the glasses on the table and then looked over at me and the money spread across the bed. Only a fellow Irishman would have brought three glasses. He then looked over at a partially dressed Miss World brushing her hair like a beautiful mermaid. I opened the champagne and gave him one of the £50 notes as a tip. He was obviously pleased with this, as the money probably represented a week's wages for him. Yet he hesitated as he tucked the note in his pocket. 'Can I ask you something, Mr Best?'

'Of course,' I said.

He looked again at Mary, looked at the money on the bed, looked at me again and his face assumed a look of genuine pity. 'Tell me Mr Best – where did it all go wrong?'

Career Highlights

⚽ *Northern Ireland international: 37 caps, 9 goals*

⚽ *2 Championships (1965 and 1967), an FA Cup (1963) and a European Cup (1968) with Manchester United*

David Platt

David Platt sits comfortably in England's top-ten all-time goalscorers. Many will remember him for exploding onto the international scene during Italia '90. England just missed out on a place in the final, but their extended stay provided David and his teammates with plenty of time to kill back at the squad headquarters.

We trained nearly every morning and then lunch would bring the highlight of the day when Brian Scott, the Football Association's travel organiser, brought in that morning's English newspapers. In the first three weeks the majority of the articles were less than complimentary.

The afternoons would be taken up by either playing cards or taking a nap. The evenings were better because there was always a match on the television, and although it may have had no bearing on us whatsoever, the fact that the majority of us had placed a bet with the squad bookmakers, 'Honest Links and Shilts', made it a lot more interesting. When there wasn't a game being played we would have a race night. Again, Gary and Peter would be the bookies, giving odds on the horse races that the physiotherapist Fred Street provided on video. Due to the fact that financially the pair of them were doing very well, Bryan Robson convinced Fred to be involved in 'The Sting'.

Fred agreed, resulting in all of us knowing that on this occasion in race five, horse number five would win. The plan was for everyone except Gazza and Pop Robson to place a bet on the other horses in the field thus making Links extend the odds on horse number five. Then, just before the off Gazza and Pop weighed in with a large wager on horse five. Fred videoed the whole scene on his camcorder as Shilt's face dropped further and further as horse five stormed to the front. For the record, Gary cottoned on immediately but then he would, wouldn't he!

Career Highlights

- England international: 62 caps, 27 goals, 8th highest England goalscorer of all time

- UEFA Cup (1993) with Juventus • Italian Cup (1994) with Sampdoria • Championship and FA Cup (both 1998) with Arsenal

Peter Marinello

Peter Marinello, a 19-year-old Scottish winger, exploded sensationally on the scene in 1970 when Arsenal paid Hibernian £100,000 for the 'new George Best' and he scored a goal at Manchester United on his debut. With his long dark hair, good looks, fashionable clothes and mod image, Marinello was at the very centre of the swinging London scene, caught up in an incredible whirlwind of drinking, discos and dolly birds. But the player-come-playboy admits he squandered his talent.

The sport of kings was my great love after football and at Arsenal I hit it off immediately with Alan Ball when he joined the club from Everton in December 1971 and we discovered a mutual love of racing.

A few years later Bally and I trotted off to Newmarket Sales and ended up paying £6,000 for a two-year-old out of Firestreak, which we decided to christen Go Go Gunner.

I organised a motley six-man consortium which also comprised Stan Flashman, the ticket tout; Nick the Greek, a great Gunners fan and restaurant owner; Bob the Mechanic, who looked after the players' cars, and a North London Bookie.

Go Go Gunner would be running in Arsenal colours, of course, red with white sleeves, and for the jockey we chose a Tartan cap, 'Marinello Tartan' Bally jokingly dubbed it.

Go Go Gunner's second race as a four-year-old ended in disaster – he won.

I was at Portsmouth now and it was May 6, 1975, three days after West Ham had beaten Fulham 2-0 in the FA Cup final, and a foul Tuesday night at Windsor with the rain lashing down.

Bally's wife was out for the evening in their Mercedes, so he reluctantly had to slum it with me in my bashed-up white £300 Mini.

He was mightily relieved no one spotted him arriving at Windsor, but disappointed when our trusted trainer informed us Go Go Gunner wouldn't like the firm going, and that we'd be throwing our money down the drain backing him, even though the services of Pat Eddery had been secured.

All of Windsor seemed to have taken the hint and we watched the odds on our pride and joy slide out to 9-2, before jumping in with a big bet on 4-1 chance Moor Lane, the second favourite.

Our faces must have been an absolute picture as we watched Go Go Gunner get up to snatch victory by half a length from Moor Lane.

continued...

Peter Marinello

continued...

Bally must have done a good fifty quid on Moor Lane, yet when the press badgered us afterwards for a quote and asked if we'd backed our horse, there was no option but to stick on a sickly false smile and lie through gritted teeth; 'Yeah, of course, we've had a bob or two.'

All six races on the card proved distinctly costly for us and by the end of the night, we had to borrow £20 off a bookie to fill the car with petrol and buy a fish and chip supper on the way home.

World Cup winner Alan Ball, Arsenal's club record £200,000 signing, and £100,000 whiz kid Peter Marinello reduced to tapping up a friendly bookie for twenty quid to get home and eat: I wonder what the press would have made of that story?

Go Go Gunner's racing career finally ended in my home city of Edinburgh where he was sent off at 12/1 for the Lothian's Handicap and trailed home ninth in the nine-runner field. Played: 25, Won 2, Lost 23. I could only sympathise.

Go Go Gunner showed great promise, but never really trained on.

A bit like me, I suppose.

Career Highlights

⚽ *Peter played for Hibs, Arsenal, Portsmouth, Motherwell, Fulham, Phoenix Inferno, Hearts and Partick Thistle between 1967 and 1984*

Terry Venables

The name of former England manager Terry Venables is synonymous with success in English football. His early coaching efforts at both Crystal Palace and QPR attracted the interest of several European clubs, and he became manager of Barcelona in 1984. 'El Tel's glamorous life in Spain was a far cry from his early playing days at Chelsea.

One Christmas during my Chelsea days, we were staying at the Norbeck Hydro in Blackpool, our normal base for games in the Northwest. A black-tie function was being held, and we stood around the edge of the ballroom watching the dancers, just to pass away the evening until it was time to go to bed. Tommy (Docherty) was in a mischievous mood, however. He was talking to a woman who had bad breath, and he made no secret of the fact, turning his head away ostentatiously whenever she spoke and putting his hand over his nose. Despite this unsubtle approach, the poor woman did not even appear to realise what he was doing. After a few minutes he asked her to dance. The floor was packed, and they quickly disappeared into the crowd as they waltzed away. By the time they came round again, Tom had tied a handkerchief over his nose and mouth, like a bandit in a Western. All you could see were his eyes, while his partner kept dancing away, staring at him with a puzzled smile on her face.

Career Highlights

❂ *England international: 2 caps, manager of England 1994–1996 and Australia 1996-1998*

❂ *League Cup (1965) with Chelsea • Spanish Championship (1985) and Spanish Cup (1986) with Barcelona (manager) • FA Cup (1991) with Tottenham (manager)*

Rob Lee

Rob Lee moved into the full-time game via non-League Hornchurch before making his mark at Charlton Athletic. It was at Newcastle United that he cemented his reputation as an energetic midfielder. He progressed to become captain of the Newcastle side, during which time he gained full international honours with England.

While I was at Newcastle, during Christmas 1998, instead of the usual fancy dress or trip up the Tyne, Stuart Pearce came up with the idea of each player putting their name into a hat, and whoever you drew out, you had to buy them a present which was relevant to how they were perceived at the club. All the presents were put into a big tub and handed out and, of course, no one knew who had sent them. Pearcey got a Zimmer frame – can't think why! Pistone got a sheep's heart from the butchers, and our German international, Didi Hamann got a copy of Hitler's Mein Kampf.

The best one of all though, which unfortunately didn't come off, was Duncan Ferguson. He drew out Nobby Solano, and Dunc tried his hardest to get hold of a real life llama. He scoured Newcastle for days trying to get one but never did. Just as well really, the gifts were handed out at Austin's, the restaurant next to our Chester-Le-Street training complex – I'm not sure what the members would have made of a llama coming into the bar.

Career Highlights

☉ *England international: 21 caps, 2 goals*

☉ *Championship runner-up (1996 and 1997), FA Cup runner-up (1998 and 1999) with Newcastle*

Teddy Sheringham

Spurs hero Teddy Sheringham left Tottenham for Manchester United in 1997 and was a key figure in their extraordinary European Cup final comeback in 1999. He was also a spiky and effective presence for England over his 51 caps, and was present on the infamous pre-Euro'96 trip to China and Hong Kong where England squad members were photographed out on the town.

W e spend a lot of our lives denying ourselves that one extra drink, one more laugh or one last prank, so when we get the chance to have fun with official approval, as we did then, we grab it with both hands.

The evening started innocently enough. We had one or two drinks and then somebody suggested we try a concoction called a Flaming Lamborghini in honour of Gazza's birthday. Several of them went down, and it was after this that things started to get a bit silly. The level of hilarity reached boiling point when Robbie Fowler, chatting to a girl at the bar, was overheard by Gazza – or so Gazza claimed – to utter the immortal line: 'Do you come here often?'

Career Highlights

⊛ *England international: 51 caps, 11 goals*

⊛ *2 Championships (1999 and 2000), FA Cup (1999) and a European Cup (1999) with Manchester United*

Peter Osgood

In a career that spanned 16 years, Peter Osgood made 560 appearances for Chelsea and Southampton, scoring 220 goals. He played in the victorious Chelsea team that beat Real Madrid in the 1971 European Cup Winners' Cup Final and he is also the owner of two FA Cup winner's medals – the second of which he won with the Saints.

In 1976 Southampton won the FA Cup and I'm proud to say I was part of the winning team. Three months after the final there was a charity fund raising event held in the Tiberius Casino in Southampton city centre, which the victorious squad were invited to attend. We were also asked to take the trophy along with us to parade around. At about quarter to twelve, when the party was in full swing and my bravado had been buoyed by a beer or two, I made a pretty outrageous bet with the captain at the time, Peter Rodrigues, that I could take the cup back to my home in Camberley, a good hour away, and spend the night in bed with it. Game on.

Myself and Jim Steele calmly walked up to the security guard on the door and said we were going outside to have some photographs taken with the trophy. He said fine and, just like that, out we went. As we furtively bundled the world's most famous piece of football silverware into the back of my Ford Capri, Jim asked if I could drop him off at home. Jim lived in the town centre and, as we headed into town, I said I thought we ought to stop for a coffee. Of course by this time, everyone was spilling rowdily out of pubs and clubs. We were soon recognized and, before long, surrounded by a huge crowd of fans and well-wishers cheering out 'good lads' and 'well done Ossie, well done Jim'. I know I shouldn't have done but I couldn't resist showing them what I had in the back of my motor. We spent the early hours of that morning with fans drinking tea and coffee out of the FA Cup, until I finally put her back in the car and drove her home.

When I woke bleary eyed the next morning and turned over to see the Cup on the pillow next to me I nearly fell out of bed. I realized that I had to get her back to the club sharpish – but not before having a little cuddle! I drove like a madman back to the training ground, where I left her outside Lawrie McMenemy's office, before dashing to the changing rooms. A little while later someone came and quietly asked me to see the boss – I have to say I feared the worst. To be fair Lawrie did yell at me and said I'd nearly given everyone at Southampton a heart attack, but, as with all things, he soon saw the funny side of it.

After all, it's not every morning you wake up in bed with the FA Cup.

Career Highlights

- England international: 4 caps
- FA Cup (1970) and European Cup Winners' Cup (1971) with Chelsea • FA Cup (1976) with Southampton

Bob Wilson

Bob Wilson's career as a goalkeeper, coach and commentator has lasted over 30 years. During his playing days he was an Arsenal hero, winning a famous double with them in 1971.

I retired from playing football for Arsenal in 1974. Two months later I began my TV sports presenting career. During one Football Focus programme on BBC's Grandstand, and very early in my new career, I had led to a video-tape story when my editor called me on my hotline phone to tell me that Joe Jordan was fit to play for Manchester United, when it was expected he would be out of action for another 2/3 weeks. 'Just tell the nation he's fit' were my orders as the previous item came to an end.

Not used to the new demands of thinking fast on my feet with words, I panicked, got caught in two minds as to what I wanted to say and as I heard the Producer shout 'Stand By, Bob,' I came out with the following:

'Just before we continue, some team news just in. We've just heard Joe Jordan has just pissed a late fatness test.'

Career Highlights

⊛ *Scotland international: 2 caps*

⊛ *Championship and FA Cup (both 1971) with Arsenal*

Garth Crooks, OBE

A snappy striker with a blistering turn of pace and scorer of some memorable goals, Garth Crooks finished his playing career in 1990 after successful periods with Stoke, Tottenham, West Brom and Charlton. Since his retirement, Garth has become an integral part of promoting grass-roots football while also being a charismatic frontline presenter for BBC's 'Match of the Day'.

I had a scoop! A 'tear up' was about to take place! There had already been a number during France '98. England and German fans had been put on notice about their bad behaviour but the word on the grapevine was that the Jamaicans were determined to have their own party in Lens main square prior to their historic World Cup match against Croatia. Their apparent intentions were simple: to kick the living daylights out of the Eastern Europeans. Only this was going to be 'Kingston, bad boy style'!

This was a big story, I was the match reporter and it was on my patch. I notified all the relevant BBC crews and positioned myself yards from the proposed action. From the moment the Jamaicans arrived, there was this thick haze hanging over the square and you were hit by this 'distinctive aroma' as they set up their commercial activity. Everyone felt great as we watched them set up stalls, sell T-shirts and offer liberal amounts of over-proof Jamaican rum to all who dared! I had a couple of shots – well it was midday and strangely enough the mixture of reggae music and booze was beginning to create a real carnival atmosphere. By the time the Croatians turned up they couldn't wait to get into the party mood, swapping shirts, dancing to Bob Marley and drinking rum chasers! The nearest thing I saw to a 'tear up' was a Croatian dancing with a female police officer. We were all naturally fascinated by that 'distinctive aroma' but we thought it best not to ask!

Career Highlights

⚽ *2 FA Cups (1981 and 1982) and a UEFA Cup (1984) with Tottenham*

⚽ *Chairman of the PFA (1988)*

Craig Brown, CBE

Craig Brown played professional football for Rangers, Dundee and Falkirk. After his retirement he worked his way up the managerial ladder to become Scotland coach and then Technical Director of the Scottish Football Association. He is one of the most entertaining men in football and enjoys a good relationship with another of the Scottish game's great characters, Ally McCoist.

One of my favourite stories involves Ally McCoist the time Rangers were playing Ajax in a Champions League away match. He was unfit and did not make the journey. Instead he was invited to be one of the commentary team for the television coverage. That morning he was in the treatment room at Ibrox with three of the Rangers apprentices. They were surprised to see him there, having expected him to travel with the team even if he was not playing.

'I am going to be seeing the game at the television studio,' Ally told them. 'I'm an expert and I'll be giving my opinions. If you look in tonight you'll see me on the screen.'

One of the lads asked him what he'd say.

'That depends on the match,' said Ally, who then decided to have a bit of fun with these young lads. 'Why? What do you want me to say?'

They laughed, but Ally pressed them and told them to pick something for him to say, and then go to the pub to watch the TV and make a few pounds by betting on him coming out with those words. The lads decided to take him up on it, and one of them, seeing a pools coupon in the room, said, 'There's one for you, Ally – say the word "coupon".'

'That's not really about football,' protested Ally, but the lad insisted. A second one looked at the diagram of a human body on the wall and told McCoist he must use the word 'tibia'. Not to be outdone, the third picked the word 'piriformis', which is a muscle on the backside.

Ally squirmed a little, but the lads jibed that he had boasted he could say anything on television so he decided to do his best, but insisted that the boys write 'piriformis' down on a piece of paper which he tore from the Daily Record – or the Daily Ranger, as he likes to call it.

Later, in the studio, the presenter, Dougie Donnelly, asked him how he thought the game would go.

continued...

Craig Brown, CBE

continued...

'Well, this is going "tibia" difficult game for Rangers, but if we win it will be a real "coupon"-buster,' said Ally, delighted that he had already managed to squeeze in two of his designated words. The third word was a real struggle, however. Eventually, about halfway through the first half, Rangers were two goals down, Paul Gascoigne had been ordered off, and there was an air of depression around the studio. He was asked for a comment and Ally as usual had the perfect response, 'this is the worst Rangers "piriformis" I've seen all season!'

Career Highlights

⚽ *Scotland manager 1993–2001*

⚽ *Scottish League Championship (1962) with Dundee*

Richard Gough

One of most popular and best-loved players in Scottish history, Richard Gough earned 61 caps for Scotland, including World Cup campaigns in 1986 and 1990. Captain of Glasgow Rangers from 1990 to 1996, he was the only Rangers player to win a medal in each of their record nine successive Championships, marking him out as a unique player and leader.

It was at Ipswich I had my first opportunity to try out for a professional club.

Not that I lasted too long there. I was told I was too small and to maybe return the following summer. My friend Mitch D'Avray was signed and he stayed there for a long time and had a successful career – but, at 15, after a month's trial I was packed off back home to South Africa. It was no one's fault because I was small at 15 and Ipswich did not want to commit themselves.

Bobby Robson was the manager then and I remember the day I scored the winner for Scotland against England at Hampden when he was international team boss. I said to him after the game: 'You won't remember me but I came over for the trials with Mitch D'Avray all those years ago....' And he told me that he did remember but I hadn't returned the following summer when he had given me that invitation.

Then, a couple of years back, Mitch had a Testimonial and I was down there and at the dinner afterwards Bobby Robson told the story again. He started off his speech by saying: 'I can still remember the day that Mitch arrived with his friend from South Africa. These two little lads had both been recommended to me and I decided to keep Mitch but let the other one go back home because he was so small. I should have kept them both because the other lad was Richard Gough!'

Career Highlights

⊕ *Scotland international: 61 caps, 6 goals*

⊕ *9-in-a-row League Championships (1989–1997), 3 Scottish Cups (1992, 1993 and 1996) and 6 Scottish League Cups (1987, 1988, 1990, 1992, 1993 and 1996) with Rangers*

Gordon Banks, OBE

He was known as the 'Banks of England', and will always be remembered for 'that' save from a Pelé header in the 1970 World Cup finals. Perhaps the greatest goalkeeper there ever was.

After I had finished my playing career, I attended a sports dinner in Manchester with a number of other famous people from the football world. We were being introduced to the audience and I was standing just behind Bill Shankly. Suddenly, he turned to me and said, 'Do you know, son, I nearly quit management because of you.'

'What do you mean Bill?' I asked.

'Well,' he said, 'when I was managing Liverpool and you were for sale at Leicester, I went to my board and told them I absolutely needed to buy one more player to complete my jigsaw – Gordon Banks. They told me that they couldn't give me any more money because there simply wasn't any. After a heated row I marched furiously back to my office and wrote out my resignation letter. I then went home and next morning came into the office and thought to myself, "C'mon Bill, it's not a bad side without Gordon Banks" and tore up the letter!'

Given his subsequent achievements domestically and in Europe, I think Liverpool fans in particular would be grateful for the great man's change of heart.

Career Highlights

⚽ *England international: 73 caps*

⚽ *World Cup (1966) • League Cup (1964) with Leicester • League Cup (1972) with Stoke*

David O'Leary

David O'Leary played almost his entire career at Arsenal, making over 700 appearances for the London club. Since moving into management he has become one of the most respected coaches in the game – a reputation that was built around his huge success at Leeds, in particular their remarkable European adventures during the 2000/01 season.

One of the traditions of European games is that the directors of both clubs, together with the UEFA officials appointed for the game, meet up at either an eve-of-match dinner or a pre-match luncheon. The managers or coaches of teams and the referee and his assistants do not normally attend, so I was delighted when my wife Joy and I were invited to be part of the pre-match formalities for Lazio's visit. The dinner took place at Harewood House, the home of our club president, Lord Harewood, who is a knowledgeable football man, a great fan of Leeds and has gained a great insight into the football industry during his lifetime. He and Lady Harewood are renowned hosts, so it was with eager anticipation that we set off for their stately home near Wetherby to meet the Roman delegation.

You could see that the Lazio hierarchy were stunned by the beautiful surroundings as well as by the excellent food and wine served at the table. It was a wonderful evening, featuring witty speeches delivered in an atmosphere of genuine bonhomie. Our chairman, Peter Ridsdale, was a great ambassador in these situations and the Lazio directors accepted the low-key nature of the game with good grace. One of them even managed to invite me in his halting English to visit Rome for their derby game against Roma. It was an invitation I took up later in the season and I have to admit that it was, as the Lazio director promised, the most incredible derby encounter I have ever witnessed. It topped even the Glasgow rivalry between Celtic and Rangers for colour, noise and passion.

I went with one of the Leeds directors and Lazio looked after us both royally. Then manager Sven Goran Eriksson and his assistant Tord Grip, did everything they could to make it a great trip. They dealt with all the arrangements for us and Sven even made a booking for us at his favourite restaurant in Rome.

Career Highlights

⚽ *Republic of Ireland international: 68 caps, 1 goal*

⚽ *2 Championships (1989 and 1991), 2 FA Cups (1979 and 1993) and 2 League Cups (1987 and 1993) with Arsenal*

Archie Gemmill

Pace was a key ingredient in making Archie Gemmill one of the finest British midfield players of his time. He won three League Championships and a European Cup medal but he is perhaps best remembered for 'that' goal against Holland in 1978 and his other heroics in a Scotland shirt.

It was the morning after the night before and I was in a hurry to get home to Derby.

Nottingham Forest's John Robertson and I had been playing in an international match for Scotland, which we won at Hampden Park, but I was eager to hit the road as soon as possible after breakfast in the team hotel.

The game in Glasgow was history now as far as I was concerned, but my son Scot was playing for his school team, Ecclesbourne, that afternoon and I was determined to get there in time for the kick-off at 2pm.

We're talking about the 1970s here and the roads on the 280 miles back to the Midlands weren't the greatest. With John safely seat-belted in the front passenger seat, I put my foot down through Dumfries – and that was a big mistake. I really should have known better.

The traffic police there were infamous for being extremely strict when it came to speeding and the next thing I knew there were blue lights flashing all over the shop to tell me I was in trouble.

John and I were quizzed about who we were, what we'd been doing and where we were heading. The cop's face turned into a smile when I revealed we had been playing for Scotland and he leant into the car to congratulate us on a splendid result.

Just for a moment, I thought we'd cracked it and he'd send us on our way with no more than a good, old-fashioned warning. Fat chance. I was booked good and proper and not only that, I was summoned to appear in person three or four weeks later in court in Dumfries which meant a round trip of over 550 miles to receive a stiff fine and penalty points on my licence.

My luck was right out because when I got back to Derby, to cap a sad and sorry day, Scot's school team were beaten.

Career Highlights

- Scotland international: 43 caps, 8 goals
- 2 Championships (1972 and 1975) with Derby County • Championship (1978) and a European Cup (1979) with Nottingham Forest

Rachel Yankey

England Women's star Rachel Yankey was the first female player to be registered as a professional when she signed for Fulham. In the 2002 FA Women's Cup Final, in front of 2.5 million BBC1 viewers, she scored a breathtaking free-kick to help Fulham beat Doncaster Belles 2-1 to lift the Cup.

A couple of days after playing in the 2002 FA Women's Cup final for Fulham, I was stopped in the street by a guy who recognized me after watching the match on TV. He complimented me on the quality of the football played, which he said had surprised him, but then he asked 'how come you only play one match a year in women's football?' One of the weirder male perceptions of the women's game ...

Career Highlights

⊛ *England international: 57 caps, 8 goals*

⊛ *2 FA Women's Cups with Arsenal (1998 and 1999) • 2 FA Women's Cups with Fulham (2002 and 2003)*

Jimmy Greaves

Jimmy Greaves was the most feared striker of his day. When joining a new club, Jimmy didn't waste time introducing himself: he scored on his debut for all his League clubs and for both the England U23s and the full England team. He also enjoyed a game of cricket.

In the summers of '57, '58, and '59 I played a lot of cricket at the request of Ron Tindall, as did Mike Harrison, Peter Brabrook, Tony Nicholas, and the Sillett brothers. Surrey always seemed to be involved in a charity game or benefit match for one of their players on a Sunday to which he would extend an invitation for us to play. There were no official cricket matches on Sundays, so these charity and benefit matches attracted sizeable attendances. More often than not they would take place at some village cricket club in Surrey and would always end with everyone having a good few pints and a singsong. I used to enjoy these games as they afforded an opportunity for me to play either with or against some of my cricketing heroes such as Alec and Eric Bedser, Tony Lock, Peter May, Jim Laker and Ken Barrington. Though the games were taken seriously, they were always played with tremendous spirit and humour, which carried on after the match and well into the night. In the pavilion of one village club I remember standing next to the great West Indies batsman Everton Weekes as we queued for tea. One of the ladies serving tea took one look at Everton's six feet plus frame and stepped back in awe.

'You're a very tall fellow, aren't you?' remarked the tea lady.

'Yes, ma'am, I am,' replied Everton.

'Just how tall are you?' the lady enquired.

'Six feet three, ma'am,' Everton informed her.

'Ooooh,' purred the woman, nudging her tea-lady companion, 'and are you all in proportion?'

'No,' replied Everton grinning, 'if I was, I'd be eleven feet six!'

Career Highlights

- England international: 57 caps, 44 goals, 3rd highest England goalscorer of all-time including a record six hat-tricks

- World Cup (1966) • 2 FA Cups (1962 and 1967) and a European Cup Winners' Cup (1963) with Tottenham

David Elleray

David Elleray was a FIFA referee from 1992 until 1999 and officiated in 78 international matches in 35 different countries. He refereed at Wembley 13 times but was unable to take part in the World Cup finals in France in 1998 due to commitments at Harrow School, where he continues his professional life as a teacher.

English football is watched throughout the world and Premier League referees get used to being recognized by all kinds of people from many countries. Paul Alcock became famous overnight when he was pushed over by Paolo Di Canio. Dermot Gallagher became well known when he was suspended for failing to send off an Arsenal player. I became known for a series of controversial decisions, including two penalties in an FA Cup final.

One summer I was refereeing at the FA Premier League Youth Festival. One afternoon, not having a game, I went to watch a match involving a team from Australia. I was strolling round behind one of the goals and, with play up the far end, the Australian goalkeeper looked at me and did a double take. 'Hey, I know you, you're the famous referee!' We all like being recognized so I smiled and nodded but was soon brought down to earth when he added, 'Yes, you're Dermot Alcock!'

Career Highlights

⊛ *A leading former FIFA and Premiership referee*

⊛ *Honorary President of the Board of the Referees' Association of England*

Alan Hansen

Until a knee injury ended his playing career in 1991, Alan Hansen was one of the greatest centre-halves to ever play the game in Britain. Since then, a keen tactical nous has made Alan a regular fixture as a 'Match of the Day' pundit.

To any new player at a football club, you ask them if they are interested in horse racing. The answer is usually yes, so you tell them that today you have a tip for Ayr. 'What is it and what time is it running, asks the new player. The horse's name is 'Open the Windows'. This line never failed. The new player would then phone up family and friends telling them about the hot tip he'd been given.

'I've got a good tip for Ayr – Open the Windows.'
Many famous footballers have fallen for it including myself.

Career Highlights

❂ Scotland international: 26 caps

❂ 8 Championships (1979, 1980, 1982, 1983, 1984, 1986, 1988, 1990), 2 FA Cups (1986 and 1989), 4 League Cups (1981, 1982, 1983, 1984) and 3 European Cups (1978, 1981, 1984) with Liverpool

Bibliography

Lyon Bell thank the contributors and publishers for their kind permission to reprint extracts from the following:

Andy Cole: The Autobiography (2000) © Andy Cole, published by André Deutsch Ltd.

The Glory and the Grief (1996) © George Graham, published by André Deutsch Ltd.

Glenn Hoddle: My 1998 World Cup Story (1999) © Glenn Hoddle, published by André Deutsch Ltd.

The Boss (2001) © John Gregory, published by André Deutsch Ltd.

Odd Man Out: A Player's Diary (1997) © Brian McClair, published by André Deutsch Ltd.

Souness: The Management Years (1999) © Graeme Souness, published by André Deutsch Ltd.

Big Fry (2001) © Barry Fry, published by HarperCollins Publishers Ltd.

Addicted (1998) © Tony Adams, published by HarperCollins Publishers Ltd.

Come in Number 37 (2001) © Rob Lee, published by HarperCollins Publishers Ltd.

Strikingly Different (2000) © Kevin Phillips, published by HarperCollins Publishers Ltd.

'Arry (1999) © Harry Redknapp, published by HarperCollins Publishers Ltd.

Sir Les (1997) © Les Ferdinand, published by Headline Book Publishing Ltd.

Psycho: The Autobiography (2001) © Stuart Pearce, published by Headline Book Publishing Ltd.

Alan Shearer: The Story so far (1998) © Alan Shearer, published by Hodder & Stoughton Ltd.

Field of Dreams: My Ibrox Years (1993) © Richard Gough, published by Mainstream Publishing Ltd.

From Voikkaa to the Premiership (2002) © Sami Hyypia, published by Mainstream Publishing Ltd.

The Real McCall (1998) © Stuart McCall, published by Mainstream Publishing Ltd.

Bald Eagle (1990) © Jim Smith, published by Mainstream Publishing Ltd.

Settling the Score (2002) © Dave Bassett, published by Blake Publishing Ltd.

The Game of My Life (2003) © Craig Brown, published by Blake Publishing Ltd.

Roy Keane (2003) © Roy Keane, published by Penguin Books Ltd.

Terry Venables: The Autobiography (1995) © Terry Venables, published by Penguin Books Ltd.

Playing Extra Time (2004) © Alan Ball, published by Sidgwick and Jackson Ltd.

Leeds United on Trial (2002) © David O'Leary, published by Time Warner Books Ltd.

Teddy (1999) © Teddy Sheringham, published by Time Warner Books Ltd.

Greavsie (2003) © Jimmy Greaves, published by Time Warner Books Ltd.

Scoring at Half Time: Adventure On and Off the Pitch (2004) © George Best, published by Ebury Press.

Bibliography

Lyon Bell made their best endeavours to contact the following publishers without success:

Jack Charlton: The Autobiography (1996) © Jack Charlton, published by Partridge Press Ltd.

Achieving the Goal (1995) © David Platt, published by Richard Cohen Books Ltd.

Trevor Brooking: Autobiography (1981) © Sir Trevor Brooking, published by Pelham Books Ltd.

Both Sides of the Border (1987) © Terry Butcher, published by A. Barker Ltd.

Tosh: An Autobiography (1982) © John Toshack, published by A. Barker Ltd.

Lyon Bell also thank Will Price for use of an extract from Peter Marinello's forthcoming autobiography 'Whatever Happened to Peter Marinello?'

More Sports Stories Coming Soon

Cricket Stories: From the Nets to the Pavilion

Rugby Stories: From the Scrum Machine to the Try Line